THE
Lyric
GENERATION

François Ricard

THE *Lyric* GENERATION

*The Life and Times
of the Baby Boomers*

Translated by Donald Winkler

Stoddart

Published in 1994 by
Stoddart Publishing Co. Limited
34 Lesmill Road
Toronto, Canada
M3B 2T6
(416) 445-3333

Canadian Cataloguing in Publication Data

Ricard, François
The lyric generation : the life and times of the baby boomers

Translation of: La generation lyrique.
ISBN 0-7737-5684-1

1. Baby boom generation.   2. Baby boom generation — Quebec
(Province).   3. Civilization, Modern — 1950–   .   4. Values.
I. Title.

HN17.5.R5213 1994   306'.09'04   C94-931316-5

Cover Design: Brant Cowie/ArtPlus Limited
Cover Illustration: Hono Lulu
Typesetting: Tony Gordon Ltd.
Printed in Canada

*Stoddart Publishing gratefully acknowledges the support of the Canada
Council, the Ontario Ministry of Culture, Tourism, and Recreation,
Ontario Arts Council, and Ontario Publishing Centre in the
development of writing and publishing in Canada.*

CONTENTS

INTRODUCTION:

A GROUP PORTRAIT

My aim here is to sketch a portrait of the men and women who are today forty to fifty years old. Although they are an integral part of what we call the baby boom, these early baby boomers also form a separate cohort, and their lives and lifestyles have unique characteristics. I want to trace the history of these men and women, to discover what kind of people they are, to understand their joys and sorrows, to assess their role in our society and culture; in short, to reconstitute their unique universe.

But while this universe may be specific to that age group, it also belongs to the rest of us. For as we will see, it has become increasingly obvious that this generation, without ever losing its sense of itself, has come to occupy the centre of society. The destinies of all other groups, whether younger or older, have played and continue to play themselves out around and in relation to it — so much so that we might say that there are two ways of belonging to this generation. In the strict sense, one must have been born between the last years of the Second World War and the beginning of the fifties. But in a wider, "ecological" sense, one need only to be living alongside it, to have felt its influence or been kept in its shadow.

I have chosen to call this particular generation the *lyric* generation, an epithet that occurred to me at the outset and later became so natural that I have not been able to give it up. I know that it lacks precision, that it has neither the simplicity nor the clarity of a rigorous definition. I believe, however, that its meaning will become clear over the course of this work. But the term will always remain somewhat unfinished and open-ended, since "lyricism" is less a descriptive category than an unstable, floating concept, poetic if you will, whose "operational" content is less important than the connotations and nuances of thought and feeling inherent within it. In fact, I am not inclined to define it too narrowly. Let us say, then, that lyricism refers both to the destiny and the consciousness peculiar to the generation that concerns me. This destiny is lyric in that misfortune has passed it by, and it has unfolded under the sign of beauty, harmony, and joy: the word *lyric,* in this sense, is the opposite of *epic.* As for the consciousness that drives this generation, lyricism implies an overwhelming innocence characterized by a limitless love of oneself, an unwavering confidence in one's values and actions, and a sense of untrammelled power over life's circumstances and over the world. In this context, the use of the word *lyric* and the meaning I lend to it owe much to novelists such as Hermann Broch, Witold Gombrowicz, and above all Milan Kundera.

"A good portrait," says Baudelaire, "resembles a dramatized biography." I have therefore organized my portrait of these children of war and the immediate postwar years by dividing their lives into three main periods. The first extends from their birth to their early adolescence — the first half of the sixties. The second, which covers roughly the next decade, encompasses their youth and initiation into the world; it is a crucial phase during which this generation gains full consciousness of itself and consolidates some of its most original and durable attributes. Then, in the mid-seventies, begins what I call the age of reality, when these newly independent young men and women take society and mould it to conform to their values and aspirations. At this point, just as my now-adult protagonists' sphere of activity has expanded, so our angle of vision must widen, and their portrait becomes everyone's portrait, a portrait of our time.

This chronological structure should not, however, mislead anyone as to the true intention of the book, which is less to tell a story than to reflect a spirit, a state of mind. The reader will not find here a detailed account of the acts and deeds of the lyric generation. Those seeking anecdotes and reminiscences had best refrain from reading. For what interests me most is how the "genius" of this generation came to be and how it has expressed itself; what experiences, discoveries, and circumstances contributed to the emergence and tenacity of the convictions, expectations, and worldview that endow its members, despite their differences, with a shared sense of belonging, a deep-rooted solidarity that distinguishes this generation from those before and since.

The portrait I am presenting is that of a soul, and thus is psychological, in the widest sense of the word. I am interested in feelings, resonances, ways of being and thinking, casts of mind, spontaneous behaviour, in what some historians call philosophies of action, that is, how one's ideas about oneself are expressed in life. These traits are not individual of course, but collective and general, insofar as they are actions and attitudes that seem to emerge from and receive the approval of this generation *as a generation,* though not necessarily of each of its members. To those who would propose exceptions to my rule, I would reply that I am painting a group portrait, and group phenomena constitute my sole subject.

My method is eclectic. Although I borrow concepts and data from history, demography, sociology, psychology, political philosophy, and anthropology, my subject belongs to none of these disciplines. I have taken many liberties, daring to practise history without established facts and references to sources, demography without statistics or graphs, sociology without polls or surveys. Were I forced to define my method, I would have to say that it is, quite simply, that of literature. My sources, the references to which I attach most importance, my manner of thinking, the sort of knowledge I am seeking, all belong to the realm of literature: to feelings and thoughts inseparable from writing, which are born by and through writing, and which find in writing their only true fulfilment. Stated otherwise, I claim for this book one designation only: that of an *essay*, that is to say a hypothesis, a *possible* and therefore provisional interpretation of experience and observation; a hypothesis pushed, however, to the limit, a sort of *idée fixe* whose expression is couched in hyperbole, which is the mode of discourse, the figure of style and thought, that suits it most naturally. What I am presenting is, above all, a partial and biased hypothesis whose analysis is run through with subjectivity and passion. For the essay, as well as literature, always refers to objects and situations in which the observer is himself implicated and compromised. Hesitantly, constantly vacillating between the use of *we* and *they*, he tries in vain to keep his distance, to strive for neutrality, never knowing if he has succeeded or if, conversely, he is getting carried away or drifting off course. But at the same time, allowing for the possibility of such excesses is what gives the essay its only opportunity to attain the form of truth that is appropriate to it.

This portrait of a generation thus is also a self-portrait. This biography, an autobiography. This essay, confessions. The lyric generation is not so much studied as reflected upon, represented in the very act of being held up for examination, for nothing better characterizes it than its fascination with itself, the attention it pays to what makes it different, and the sense it has of its own vastness. That is why the confessions of a child of the lyric generation can only be — as are these — collective confessions.

But these are above all *critical* confessions, as all confessions inevitably are. I have not been complacent about my generation. Some will even find that I have denigrated it. But in the end my intention is neither to judge nor to weigh in the balance. I want only to describe and to understand, to analyze the lyric generation's spirit and impact on the world. To do so, it has often been necessary to contrast the lyric generation with those that preceded it, and thus to recall what the world and life must have been like in times past, before the lyric generation came on the scene and took control. I would prefer (without, of course, deluding myself on the subject) that these evocations of the past be seen not as nostalgia for vanished artifacts and customs, but for what they are first and foremost: a placing in perspective, the better to grasp the distinctive traits of this generation, which has itself proclaimed that rupture — and therefore confrontation with the past — be one of its touchstones and defining features.

That said, I am perfectly aware of how maddening the concept of a generation can be. Among all our determining factors, there are few so fundamental in nature and about which we can do so little. We can change our social class, language, religious affiliation, or civil status; we can exile ourselves from our native land; we can even, if need be, trade off or transform the culture we have inherited; but we can do nothing about our age or the date of our birth.

In this respect, generation is a determining factor of considerable weight, one that is biological in character, a bit like our gender or the colour of our skin. But unlike these, it is at the same time a historical factor determined in large part by the will or desire of men. An individual's generation is not only linked to a particular age group, but is also a point of anchorage in the flow of history, for human generations are born one from the other, and their succession is not regulated only by the laws of conservation or equilibrium in nature, as is the case with propagation in animals or sexual distribution; they must also obey and constantly contend with historical evolution: that part of their destiny that men create for themselves or inherit from those who came before them.

Most often, demographic equilibrium is so stable or changes so slowly that the influence of generations is barely perceptible. Indeed, everything takes place as though societies had some kind of regulating mechanism to ensure that the distribution of different age groups remains relatively constant and that, as a result, the relationships between the groups are equally stable. Under these "normal" conditions, the demographic factor goes unnoticed, and plays no significant role; it becomes, as it were, invisible, or of secondary importance. Each generation follows the same path as the one before it and passes through the different stages of life in more or less the same way.

All bets are off when this equilibrium is suddenly upset and the customary relationship between the different generations is disturbed. Now the demographic factor takes centre stage, not only in the overall evolution of society, but in the lives and minds of individuals. Those who, under ordinary circumstances, would have defined themselves in terms of any other factor than the generation to which they belong, now come to regard as fundamental that aspect of their identity and to make it the measure, at least in part, of their behaviour or of the meaning of their lives. As each generation distinguishes itself according to its own fate and experience and sets itself up in opposition to all the others, age becomes a new source of division between social groups and determines in large part the nature and progress of their relationships with one another.

We are now, it seems to me, in the midst of one such period. Our society has experienced — and continues to experience — a profound upheaval in the traditional makeup of its population, with the appearance, during and after the Second World War, of a generation whose life experience, education, and cast of mind, not to mention its very magnitude, have made it impossible for the rest of society to absorb, leaving society no other choice than to transform itself, to make room for the interloper and to respond to its needs and aspirations.

In these times of demographic disruption, whose effects will take an eternity to dissipate (if ever), we are faced with this new challenge: to understand our generation, to take note of our "statistical condition," as Valéry would put it, and thus, perhaps, to transcend it.

Part One

A LUCKY STAR

TO BE BORN AT THE DAWN
OF THE WORLD

Twenty years ago, we had no hope for
the future; now we are afraid of nothing.

Alexis de Tocqueville
L'Ancien régime et la révolution

To belong to the lyric generation is to come into the world
in joy. When I try to imagine the climate in which we were
conceived by our parents, the image that comes to my mind
is one of freshness and light: it is a sort of morning for the
world.

The war was over and our parents demobilized at last.
They were the conquerors who, along with their allies, had
succeeded in humbling the enemy and warding off evil; their
values of liberty, tolerance, and piety had prevailed. They were
the new masters whose task it would be to build the future.
For our parents, as for all citizens of North America, the
euphoria of victory was pure and free of bitterness. Unlike
Europeans, their lands had been spared the horror of combat,

their dead and wounded were fewer in number, and no ruins — material or moral — surrounded them. Their homes were intact and their consciences, for the time being at least, were clear; they bore no responsibility either for death camps or collaboration with the enemy. The world could begin again without delay; it would be their world, one they had unknowingly been hoping for and dreaming of for a very long time.

The sense of relief that marked those years was not due only to victory and the return of peace, but even more to the fact that the ten infinitely more difficult years that preceded the war had come to an end. The Depression had been an interminable period of moral and economic disorder, of repressed or thwarted hopes, of humiliation and discouragement.

In fact, compared to this darkness, the war was a form of salvation to our parents, as Gabrielle Roy's *The Tin Flute*, published in 1945, shows so well. Of course, because of the "war effort," everything was rationed, controlled, and regulated, so that on the surface life seemed no different from what it had been during the Depression. But despite the deprivation, scarcity, and constraints, times had changed. Thanks to the military industries and production destined for the allied countries, it was easy to find work, and money was circulating again. Of course, that money couldn't be spent, but it could, at least, be saved for the future. In other words, it was now possible to hope for better days; life was beginning again.

The Second World War, in fact, presented this paradox: while it was a nightmare for those who bore the brunt of its sorrows and devastation, for others it was a veritable emancipation, putting an end to the Depression and jump-starting the economy. Such was the case in Canada, where the war years represented a period of plenty, marked by a return of prosperity on the one hand, and by social, political, and cultural ferment on the other. In Quebec the war years were so intense, so unprecedented, and broke so completely with the gloom and insecurity of previous years that historians have seen that period as a kind of Quiet Revolution before its time. The climate was one of change and daring. The rural population, which the Depression had kept on the land, once again began to move to the cities. Women entered the work force in huge numbers. Workers organized, and demanded their rights with more determination than ever. The young discovered American music and film. Writers and artists, freed from the control of the clergy, were receptive to new styles and ideas. The desire for liberty and renewal was felt everywhere. It was taken for granted that the world was no longer the same and that a new age was being born.

Of course, there was still a great deal of uncertainty, for the salvation offered by the war, however real it may have been for the time being, provided no guarantees; it would perhaps last no longer than the conflict. Once peace was re-established and the factories had no more tanks or bombs to manufacture, would everything collapse once more? Would the world be plunged into a depression even worse than the one that had just ended?

On the contrary, the postwar years prolonged and even intensified the miracle. The dreaded layoffs did not take place, the misery and unemployment did not return, and the rationing did come to an end. And little by little the conditions for, and early signs of, abundance became more and more entrenched (true abundance would have to wait a few years for the economy to complete its conversion). There was a thawing out, an easing of existence, as that trust in the future that had made its first tentative appearance during the war grew steadily stronger and more confident, and would soon become unshakeable.

We have no idea, today, of the force and the novelty of this feeling. It coincided with and set the tone for our birth, however, and we must try to imagine it as best we can.

For years, our parents had lived hand to mouth, curbing their desires and hoping for nothing more than the strength or good fortune to muddle through, to sort things out, to keep from falling by the wayside. The youngest among them, those whose adolescence coincided with the Depression and whose twentieth birthdays fell during the war, had become accustomed not only to having nothing, but to expecting nothing, or ever so little; they asked of life only the bare necessities and the strength to hang on to the little that had been accorded them. As for the oldest, who had been hit by the disaster of 1929 while they were adolescents or young adults and had seen their lives or careers shattered by it, they had been dogged ever since, sometimes by regret, sometimes by resignation, but always by the expectation of the worst. In either instance, it is easy to imagine what the mood at the end of the war and during the first postwar years must have meant to them. What an unforeseen godsend, what an awakening, as though huge shutters had suddenly burst open to let the air and the light stream in.

Nothing in their past could have prepared them for the happiness that was available to them now, a happiness no longer restricted to small groups as was the case before the Depression and the war, but accessible to everyone, or at least to a much larger segment of society. A combination of comfort, security, and amenities of all sorts, it was a democratic happiness to which all could legitimately aspire. Everyone had a right to the *possibility* of happiness, to the promise of a life that would not only be free from deprivation and hardship, but that would constitute a movement onwards and upwards, of continual and potentially unlimited progress. The world, which up to that point had been a sort of trap, now offered the prospect of boundless opportunity.

It is strange that historians in Quebec refer to this period as *la grande noirceur,* or the "age of darkness." Perhaps it is because they are preoccupied only with politics, or because they are themselves part of the lyric generation, or its victims. In fact, if we look at the postwar years from a more radical, yet more concrete perspective — an *existential* perspective — they appear, on the contrary, to have been bathed in light. An overwhelming, triumphant light that beamed down and banished in a trice the former darkness, utterly transforming the tenor of existence. Now, with everything in life so altered, where did that leave governments and their institutions? What could they do, when, for the time being at least, they were themselves unchanged?

It is in the context of that radiance, then, that we must imagine the birth and early childhood of the lyric generation. Better still, think of this generation as being conceived by the brightness itself. From our very beginnings in that historical moment, we were the sons and daughters of this morning light that was spreading over the world.

Let us return once more to our parents and this feeling of sudden joy that the times inspired, and which they experienced so intensely in the life they were living, if not in their consciousness. Something at the same time told them it was not truly theirs. Children of the Depression and the war, they felt somehow unworthy of the world that was beginning, or poorly prepared, or already too old, even though many were not yet twenty-five. It was a time of desire, of aspiration, and they had not been taught how or to what they should aspire; they did not know what a life ruled by desire and expectation was like. They were neither disappointed nor despairing. Far from it: the world that was in the making filled them with delight. But something told them that they were not really made for such marvels.

This at least is how I prefer to understand that singular logic by which our parents chose to give birth to us rather than keep everything for themselves. Procreation was their way of adapting to the situation, of expressing the joy and the confidence the times had bestowed on them. This land of promise had to be populated; happiness having finally become a possibility, it was essential, short of seizing it for themselves, or perhaps in order to seize it all the more surely, to settle it with new beings that came from them but were cut from a different cloth, beings that were innocent and therefore able to feel at home in this new land.

This strategy, or rather this wager, would within a few years materialize into a striking phenomenon — the baby boom, whose nature and evolution I describe in the chapters that follow. For the moment, I would like to focus on the *triggering mechanism* of this phenomenon, for it marks the appearance of the lyric generation, the initial surge, the first battalion of what would little by little become a gigantic army of baby boomers.

But I do not think it is possible to get a fair idea of the origins of this generation or attain a true understanding of its genius without some reference, at the very start, to the contribution made by the unique state of mind bestowed on our parents by the times in which they lived. For these men and women to decide to dedicate their lives so completely to their children, their sense of deliverance and their faith in the future must have been singularly powerful.

Paradoxically, they must also have been inspired by a kind of despair, or at least a pessimism with regard to what they had been and what they had experienced, a sense that their own lives had gone awry and arrived at an impasse. This impasse was called the Depression and the war; it was called poverty, disorder, enmity, the horrors of the battlefield. Under these conditions, only one redemption was possible, only one revenge: to opt for an innocent and therefore absolutely new future, for change and a forgetting of the past. Where they themselves were concerned, these adults knew that innocence could not be regained. But children, given enough time, enough room, and the necessary freedom, really could forget and begin again.

Custom dictates that we have children in order to pass on what we have received, or to ensure that the world we know will endure. But these parents had their children precisely because they knew or felt that they would *not* pass on the world in which they had lived, because this world was *not* going to endure, and what is more, because they wanted to ensure that that world would not endure. The period that was beginning was to have nothing in common with the Depression and the war, nor with an older past. It was the need to bring about this new world and a desire for change rather than perpetuation that drove them to have children in such great numbers and so soon.

Traditionally, children have embodied the future. But this future, somehow, has always been viewed as the preservation or the extension of the present. Certainly, it was expected that the new generation would do better than their fathers and mothers, and that in their hands the patrimony they had received would be enriched. But, basically, their role was to pick up where others had left off, to keep the faith, and to prolong, through their own lives, the lives of their parents. They were there to ensure that death and time not prevail, that the world into which they were born remain as it had been when it was entrusted to them.

For the lyric generation, things were both similar and

utterly different: similar in that, like all children, its members were also put in charge of the future, but different, and radically so, because the future had a whole new meaning. Rather than being the outgrowth or consolidation of the present, it was to be its negation, a time about which nothing was yet known other than that it could only be different from and infinitely better than the current state of affairs. The past and the present, on the one hand, and this future, on the other, had nothing in common, so that forging a world for the future could only happen by doing away with the current and past worlds, by exceeding accepted limits, by rejecting tradition.

That is why the newborn had never before to this degree been invested with all the magic inherent in the very idea of birth, the symbol of new beginnings, new flowering, renewal. Like anything imprinted on the self so early on, before consciousness and one's critical faculties can intervene, this first definition would be decisive. From the start it mapped out this new generation's existence, or at least those major axes that would provide the orientation for their lives. It decreed the rules and furnished a model or ideal that would be the standard against which they would measure the meaning and value of their lives, determine their success or failure, decide whether or not they had been true to themselves.

This primal definition made them responsible for carrying out a mission. Both positive and negative, this mission called for them not only to build the future, but also to refuse to prolong the past. These pure and infinitely light "interlopers," who had no memory and no ties, who were blameless and free of all hurts, like princes whose kingdoms were not yet of this world, were loosed upon the world to break with what had been and to instigate what was to come. Mandated by their parents to be the first inhabitants of a new world, they would leave the dead to bury the dead and destroy or turn away from the past to dedicate themselves to one task only: the invention of a new world and a new life.

And that is why the term *lyric generation* suits them so well. In Milan Kundera's vocabulary, one of the essential components of lyricism is precisely the attitude of seeing the world as an immense open field, as raw material that poses no obstacle to individuals, so that they can take it apart and remake it as they please in their own image and for their own fulfilment, without hindrance and without compromise. Amnesia and despoilment do not give peace to the lyric spirit, because its primary goal is not to do away with anything. Destruction is not its intent. It is there to prepare a (new) beginning, the inauguration of a world of plenty whose imminence and practicability are, in its view, guaranteed. It is thus an *innocent* desire, and therefore terrible. Before it, all the world can do is brace itself.

STRENGTH IN NUMBERS

> They have numbers, and therefore
> real power, on their side.
>
> Hannah Arendt
> *Crises of the Republic*

Apart from the historical context and the existential climate that surrounded — and in a sense, determined — the birth of the lyric generation and that foreshadowed its unique psychology and the broad lines of its future, another important factor must be considered if we want to understand just how this destiny would be fulfilled and appreciate the charmed life this generation would lead for decades to come. This factor is not moral or ideological in nature, but is rather material and elementary — biological — since it concerns a phenomenon known as the *baby boom*.

We must not confuse what demographers and historians mean when they use this term with what I call the lyric generation. The two are neither the same nor opposite, but have a more subtle relationship that must be grasped correctly if we want to understand the distinctive features of the lyric generation itself.

The baby boom is usually defined as lasting fifteen or twenty years, or up to the beginning of the sixties. But opinions differ as to when, exactly, it began, some opting for the war, others for immediately after the war. Although it makes very little difference, I prefer the first definition, according to which the baby boom got under way as soon as the birth rate, after having fallen steadily for a dozen years, began to mount rapidly and significantly, reaching levels approximating those known before the Depression. Such a reversal did indeed take place during the war, or more specifically during the second half of the war. It was in 1942–43 that the movement took off, and the resulting demographic marvel would endure for twenty years.

Born during the war and immediately after the war, the lyric generation does not represent the baby boom as a whole, or even the majority of its members, but the very beginnings of the movement, what demographers would call its first cohorts. The lyric generation was the prelude to the baby boom.

These first-born baby boomers were not necessarily the firstborn of their family, of course, although many of them were. In fact, two main groups made up the lyric generation.

The first group consisted of the eldest of the family. They form a particularly numerous contingent because of the large number of marriages that took place at that time, not only of young couples, but also of older couples who had delayed getting married because of the Depression and the war. These couples, possessed of a kind of impatience to procreate, had their first child very soon after marriage.

The other main group encompasses those children — little afterthoughts — that appeared unexpectedly, as though by miracle, at a time when the family seemed already complete. There were sometimes more than one, and they formed a sort of second family younger than the first. Their relationships with older siblings were rather distant, and their connection with parents quite different from that experienced by the older children. Although they had the same father and mother, there was a generation of difference between them. The fact is, the "logic" that prevailed at their birth was not the same. While their brothers and sisters were children of the Depression, these "second brood" children were born not out of necessity, but by virtue of a kind of grace, in tune with the spirit of the times. It was not unusual for them to have nephews or nieces their own age. Perhaps their parents had wanted to follow in the steps of their own older sons and daughters, and to play a role, despite their relatively advanced age, in the new world that was beginning.

But whether they were the eldest or the youngest, these children of the war and the immediate postwar period often enjoyed privileged status at the centre of their families. To be born before or after all the others not only set them apart and imprinted this distinctiveness on their consciousness, it also merited them special care and a very special attachment to their parents. For in contrast to their older brothers and sisters, and much more than their younger siblings, these cherished children represented in their purest state all the symbolic trappings of change and rebirth associated with the end of the forties. They were the ones who were born at the precise moment when the sun had set on the ruins of the old world and a new day was dawning to herald a new age. Certainly, the climate of confidence, of wonderment even, that I described in the previous chapter would continue to make itself felt in the years to come, but never as intensely as in those first days. Just being born at such a moment, bathed in a light so pure, already constituted for these children an incalculable blessing, whose benefits they would reap first in their childhood and youth, and then for all the rest of their lives.

Even if the baby boom had not taken place, the children born towards the end of the war or just afterwards would surely have been marked by the new mood that accompanied prosperity and the return of peace. But those children would have been just another postwar generation, as short-lived and easily assimilated as its predecessors. The crucial difference, in the case of the lyric generation, derives from the fact that it was ushering in a vast movement soon to be known as the baby boom. Far from remaining isolated, these children would be followed by a multitude of other children, born all through the fifties and infused like them, though to a lesser degree, with the new spirit of the times.

This fact is paramount. It provided the lyric generation with an immense strategic advantage, giving it an impact it never would have had on its own, one that far outstripped that of any previous generation. Sheer numbers made the baby boom unavoidable. By abruptly increasing the proportion of children and young people in society, that is, of one specific age group to the detriment of others, it would radically alter the traditional balance of that society. As a result, it created a situation that was not only unusually amenable to upheavals, but one that would also give this particular age group, if only because of its numerical weight, enormous influence and authority, while diminishing that which had long been the prerogative of older groups.

The lyric generation would forever have the support and added clout of those numberless troops drawn from the baby boom's younger battalions, in whose name it would speak and whose authorized representative it would hold itself to be.

Thus the presence of the lyric generation in the world, its mission, and the claims and demands it would argue before its elders would all be reinforced and legitimized by the gigantic mass movement of which it was itself the advance party, and for which, in fact, it was blazing the trail.

If we cannot equate the baby boom with the lyric generation, we can say that without the former, the latter would never have had the means to impose itself as it was able to do. It could not have secured so easily the central position it occupied from a very young age, nor could it have freed itself so completely from the influence of earlier generations, which, constrained by the simple law of numbers, would have no choice but to retreat before it. In short, without in itself constituting the baby boom, the lyric generation had the advantage of being both its avant-garde and its elite corps.

Given the lyric generation's debt to the baby boom, we should give some serious attention to a phenomenon that represents a key event in contemporary history, one whose repercussions are infinitely broader and deeper than we are inclined to believe. In particular, I would like to stress the *abnormality* of the baby boom, and thus its unpredictable and disturbing nature. To do so I must cite some of the interpretations that specialists in these matters — sociologists, demographers, and historians, all people infinitely more competent than I — have chosen to give to this phenomenon. I must myself adopt the role, in a sense, of defender of the baby boom, since many of these same specialists tend to dispute, if not its reality, at least its abnormality.

THE BABY BOOM AS RUPTURE

What, in the final analysis, is the baby boom?

Essentially, it consists of the rapid and sustained increase in the number and rate of births that took place in certain countries, including Canada, beginning around the end of the Second World War.

But the most important aspect of the baby boom — that which made it a major historical event — is not so much the birth rate itself, but the contrast between its rise and the trend prevailing up to that point: the decrease in birth rate observed since the beginning of the Depression and even the middle of the nineteenth century. It was from this *relative* point of view that the onset and persistence of the baby boom represented such a decisive demographic event; it was utterly atypical and unlike what had been expected. Suddenly the long trend of fewer and fewer births was reversed. The maternity wards were bursting at the seams, the photographers were making fortunes, and the newborn were issuing forth like inexhaustible manna. The rupture between this world teeming with children and the old one where they were few and far between could not have been clearer. And as we will see throughout this book, that rupture brought consequences that were both far-reaching and decisive.

Ruptures and anomalies, however, are anathema to specialists in the social sciences, who are trained to demonstrate that everything — even the most astonishing and seemingly unprecedented — is perfectly normal, foreseeable, and in no way surprising if it is viewed from the right perspective.

And that is exactly what has transpired in the case of the baby boom. While at first acknowledging how unusual the phenomenon was, demographers and historians then insisted, in order to account for it in a way that was satisfactory to them, on going beyond this appearance, or simply doing away with it altogether. This they did by slotting it into the category of "tendencies" or "series" that are more "long-term."

Although more often than not these explanations obscured the true significance of the baby boom, it is worthwhile looking at them briefly, for they help shed light on the distinctive features and meaning of the boom.

The first and most simplistic way to rob the baby boom of its significance is to show that the birth rate during those fifteen or twenty years was far from representing an all-time record, that it was much lower than those of the past and barely reached the levels observed just prior to the Depression. However accurate such an attempt may be, this nuance must be qualified by two observations. First, we must remember that the postwar rise in the birth rate was accompanied, thanks to advances in hygiene and medicine, by a much diminished infant and juvenile mortality rate, so that a birth rate equal to or even lower than that of former times would indeed produce a greater number of children.

And second, even if we could establish that the baby boom produced fewer babies than an earlier comparable period (the years known as the "revenge of the cradle" in

Quebec, for instance), one crucial fact remains: compared with the period that immediately preceded it (the years of the Depression and the beginning of the war), the baby boom represented a quantitative leap as undeniable as it was spectacular. It doesn't matter whether or not it constituted a historical record. What counts, if we want to understand the cast of mind and the behaviour of this new generation, is its relationship with the population that was *contemporary* with it, in other words, with the other generations living at the same time and with which it was in direct contact, and in particular, the generation immediately preceding it. In this context, the disparity could not be more extreme, nor could the numerical superiority of the baby boom be more overpowering.

Another interpretation, more interesting than the first, also restricts itself to these two periods — the ten years of the Depression plus the fifteen or twenty of the baby boom — and sees the latter period as a simple consequence of catching up or of compensation. The high birth rate of the postwar era was a natural reaction to the losses incurred due to the low rate since the beginning of the thirties, and the baby boom was the result of a kind of homeostatic regulation, not unlike the broad laws of conservation that govern nature. In fact, it is possible, if we project the evolution of the birth rate onto a long-term diachronic curve, to observe a rather good correspondence or reciprocal relation between the crest of the baby boom and the trough represented by the ten or fifteen preceding years. From such a large perspective, this trough and crest do not radically alter the overall equation, and in fact cancel each other out.

So they say. Nevertheless, however accurate this interpretation and the calculations on which it relies and however comforting in appearance the understanding it provides, this explanation, once more, misses the point. The baby boom did indeed make it possible to replenish the population's "stock" of individuals after it had been depleted as a result of the Depression and the war. But this purely quantitative renewal had a profound effect on the *composition* of the population, because the children who came into the world during the fifties did not replace the children who had not been born during the Depression; rather, they replaced the *adults* that these children would have become, which is not at all the same thing.

My aim here is not to impugn the value or the usefulness of a historical or demographic approach. All I am saying is that the neutral and abstract approach so important to science has limited validity when applied to the raw material of history, by which I mean the motivations and perceptions that inspire the thoughts and acts of the participants themselves, especially where current or recent history is concerned. Historians, for example, can teach all about the cyclical character of crises and periods of prosperity or observe the gradual progress of urbanization, but nothing can change the fact that every economic depression represents a dramatic rupture in the lives of its victims, and that each family that sells its land and moves to the city does so for reasons and under circumstances that for it are unique. From the perspective of history as lived day to day, with its limited horizons, its deep contradictions, and its shifting parameters, no curve appears stable; the crests are mountains, the troughs abysses. Made up neither of continuity nor of long-term trends, but of constant deviations, ruptures, and sometimes revolutions, the curve reflects the ever unpredictable history of our joys and sorrows, our hopes and failures — the true history of our life and death.

To grasp its *ultimate* significance, we must of course make an effort to see it in a more general context, and that honour falls to history. But such an understanding will be all the richer if, in the quest for enlightenment, history does not relegate to the shadows this raw material that provides an *immediate* sense of events and circumstances, and that constitutes the meaning given to their universe by the very people who inhabited it.

I apologize for this digression. Its aim was to clarify the point of view I have adopted in this book and, to come back to the subject of this chapter, to explain just why it is so inadequate to interpret the baby boom as a minor demographic incident in the long-term evolution of natality. For, however "foreseeable" the baby boom may prove to be from an overall perspective, in the final analysis it will never be anything more than an *a posteriori* prediction. If, on the contrary, we immerse ourselves in the period and try to recapture the immediacy and context of the experiences and perceptions themselves, then the baby boom appears in a quite different light: as the reversal of a situation, a change that was rapid and utterly unexpected, the end of one state of affairs that had been constant for fifteen years, and the beginning of another that was completely different. And even if this deviation appears illusory in the light of long-term constants, it still represents the deepest meaning of the baby boom, its primary existential truth.

The same reasoning would apply to another expert analysis, the most serious of those dealt with here. For this analysis does not restrict itself, like its predecessors, to proving that the baby boom was an anomaly in appearance only and a function of mere circumstance. It denies categorically that there was any perturbation or change in direction whatsoever.

The argument this time is based on another parameter: fertility. If we calculate the total fertility of all mothers who gave rise to the baby boom, we see that the number of children they had had by the end of their productive lives did not demonstrate spectacular growth, but barely exceeded the total observed in their own mothers' generation. Which is to say that the general decline in fertility since at least the nineteenth century was not interrupted by the baby boom but continued almost unchanged, so that the baby boom appears as a simple epiphenomenon of this major trend.

And yet, the rise in the number of newborn that characterizes the baby boom is undeniable. This apparent contradiction between the idea of rupture (a birth explosion) and the idea of continuity (a stable or decreasing fertility rate) can be explained by the rapidity with which the mothers of the baby boom produced their offspring. Not only did these women give birth to their first child very soon after marriage, but they barely paused before having subsequent children, so that the interval between births was brief. Then, however, deciding that three or four little ones made for a large enough family, these same women stopped having children at a rather young age. So they did not, in fact, have more children than their mothers, but their fecundity was so rapid, so concentrated over a short period of time, that this concentration produced that sudden, apparently disorderly inflation of the birth rate that we call the baby boom.

And that, to my mind, is the crucial factor. Long-term fertility curves may betray no significant or enduring variation, but it is nonetheless true that life in the forties and fifties was deeply marked by the invasion of this horde of children. And no analysis, however broad in scope, will ever entirely succeed in neutralizing the baby boom's unsettling and unforeseen impact on what demographers call the "age pyramid"; gone was the equilibrium that had long been familiar.

As the advance wave of the baby boom, the lyric generation made its debut in the world as an abnormality. Born of an upheaval, of an abrupt reversal in trends, it would go on to recreate and amplify, again and again, that which brought it into being: rupture itself.

CHILDREN OF FREEDOM

The analysis based on fertility does, however, have one merit: it highlights an important factor that contributed to the mood prevailing at the outset of the baby boom and coinciding with the appearance of the lyric generation. Indeed, in this curious pattern of procreation that our parents adopted, this rapidity with which they gave birth to their children, we can detect the outward signs of what can only be called a kind of *freedom*.

For if our mothers had fewer children than their own mothers, it is not only because they began a little later, it is also because they stopped earlier and at a relatively young age, an age when they could still have given birth. While their mothers continued to bring children into the world until they were past forty, ours, for the most part, ceased doing so around the middle or even at the beginning of their thirties. And it is this precocious interruption, this decision they made, before nature obliged them to do so, of calling a halt to any increase in the number of their offspring that is indicative of our parents' freedom. Now, if they were able at that point in their lives to choose to have no more children, is it not possible that they had made a similar choice, and exercised a similar sort of freedom, in giving birth earlier on to the children they had?

Certainly, tradition and the church urged them to marry and to procreate abundantly. And certainly, many women who had worked in the war industries had been encouraged if not forced to return home and resume the role of wife and mother. But social control and ideology fall short of providing an adequate explanation.

One explanation that feminists offer sees the baby boom as nothing more than another sign of the exploitation and suppression of women at that time. The postwar period, they say, propagated an image of women that appeared to break with traditional stereotypes, but in reality only perpetuated them beneath a facade of modernity. This new feminine mystique — the glorification of conjugal love, the importance of caring for the body, a taste for a comfortable life, and personal fulfilment, as well as a more "modern" philosophy of childhood education — was only one more trap set for women by the good old phallocratic power structure. Encouraged to see themselves as different from their backward mothers and to embrace a new style of life, women were, in fact, still being urged to dream only of marriage and pregnancy, and to submit meekly to the authority of their husbands. And the baby boom was an obvious symptom of this consecration of inequality, of this enduring subjugation of women. In other words, our mothers were no different from all mothers since the beginning of time and had brought children into the world without really having wanted to.

The feminist vision has imposed itself so strongly on society that we accept this type of explanation as self-evident. Even women who are now older than sixty will, when asked about the past, agree with such an interpretation and say that they had no choice whether or not to have their children — the children of the baby boom. But however sincere and well-meaning it may be, does such an account, given after the fact, really reflect what actually happened? Do we not see here, to a large degree, the effect of current feminist thinking? Have these women, influenced by their own daughters, been led to reevaluate their lives and to reinterpret them from a point of view that corresponds more to today's way of seeing things than to the reality of what they experienced and what they felt when they were young? Such a revision of the past, such amnesia, is perfectly comprehensible if we take into account the effect the lyric generation had on all of society. It is, in fact, a relatively benign ramification.

However that may be, attributing the baby boom to the subjugation of women, or in more general terms, to conjugal "alienation" makes little sense in light of certain facts. The first is that the baby boom was not more conspicuous in Quebec; it was if anything a little less so than in other societies such as English Canada, Australia, and above all the United States, where Catholic and traditionalist influences were much weaker and contraception more widely accepted. Besides, if the baby boom was merely a symptom of the exploitation of women, why was it virtually nonexistent in other countries where sexual inequality was certainly not less acute? Were Spanish, Italian, and French women any more liberated and less subjected to "male power" than those living in America? If this seems unlikely, why then did they not fall into the "trap" of chronic pregnancy as well?

But let's get back to Quebec and consider once more the years that preceded the baby boom, in particular, the Depression. Conservative attitudes towards women and the influence of the Church and traditional elites, with their gospel of fertility, were certainly as dominant then as after the war. Indeed, in the atmosphere of moral uncertainty that characterized these years and gave rise to an important revival of religious and nationalist fervour, they had considerable force and authority. And yet, during these same years, marriages and births fell sharply. In other words, no matter how "alienated" they were, however imbued with religious principles and obedient to their priests, couples in those difficult times were quite capable of managing their own sexuality and resisting injunctions to reproduce. No matter how much priests expounded the sacred duty of procreation and promised hellfire if such commandments were ignored, men and women still found ways not to thrust into the rotten world around them as many children as were asked of them.

Now, since these couples — and these women — were able to express their freedom under such extreme social control, how could they not have done so when new circumstances were undermining the power and prestige of traditional authority and acting against the established view? There was the rural exodus and rampant urbanization, the increase in information, and the rapid development of new means of communication, a wider knowledge of what was being done and thought in other countries, the experience of factory and office work for a whole generation of young women, and so on. In short, the potential for freedom after the war had become greater than ever, and yet the baby boom, this epidemic of marriages and childbirth, nevertheless took place.

I am not presenting myself as an apostle of procreation. All I am saying is that there is no reason to think that our parents or our mothers, because they had no access to the pill, the IUD, therapeutic abortion, or divorce, or because the world of work outside the home was largely closed to them, necessarily had their children under duress and without really choosing to do so. Certainly, modern means of contraception, as well as access to careers and employment, are undeniable instruments of both personal and sexual freedom, and their absence seriously limits this freedom. But that does not mean that freedom is eliminated completely and that our parents were chained to reproduction like beasts of the forest. Acting in a certain way, even when the possibilities of not doing so are limited, does not mean one is not acting freely. In any case, the scale and suddenness of the baby boom, and the clean break it represented, can only be explained if we accept that one way or another it resulted from a conscious choice on the part of the adults of the time.

And this, too, may be considered one of the privileges of that generation. For perhaps the first time in history, especially in Quebec, children were being conceived as the result of free choice and love and not primarily out of duty or necessity. Certainly, our parents, in marrying and giving birth to us, found themselves conforming to the commands of the old conjugal moral authority. But that was not their primary motivation. The moral and ideological climate even then would have allowed them to abstain. And yet they did not. Children had long ceased to represent any sort of economic resource, and had become an almost endless financial burden. And yet, against all logic, our parents assumed this burden. Even though not having children was less of an option for them than it would later be for us, it definitely was an option. And they did not take advantage of it.

THE BABY-BOOM EFFECT
AND QUEBEC

Before focusing all my attention on the lyric generation itself, I must say one last word about the baby boom, and the impact it may have had in the special case of Quebec. Curiously, its impact was at once less pronounced and more spectacular in Quebec than elsewhere.

As we know, the baby boom was not felt everywhere equally. Without our knowing exactly why, it was concentrated in a number of specific countries — Canada, Australia, New Zealand, and the United States. The only traits these countries seem to have had in common was that, first, they were former British colonies and, second, their principal national territory had not been seriously affected by the destruction of the Second World War. But it is hard to see the connection between the baby boom and these two factors, or why other countries with these features — Ireland, Jamaica, South Africa — did not share in the baby boom, at least not to the same degree. According to some specialists, the baby boom occurred in "young" countries. But what does that mean? Are the United States and Canada younger than Argentina or Brazil? How does one measure the age of a country? For the time being, it seems, we must accept the fact that we can find no satisfactory explanation.

Although part of a country belonging to the select group, Quebec was less affected than the rest of Canada and the other countries by the phenomenon. Certainly, Quebec's birth rate as of the Second World War is comparable to the rate in countries that in which a baby boom occurred, but since Quebec's birth rate in the past, and especially over the previous fifteen years, had been higher than elsewhere, the increase appeared, and was, less extreme. In other words, because Quebec had not lost the habit of having children, it was taken less unaware by their sudden profusion.

We should not, however, deduce from that, as some have done, that the upheaval in Quebec as a result of the baby boom was negligible, or that it was less noteworthy than in societies where it occurred on a larger scale. In the beginning, perhaps, the abundance of children might have appeared to be a simple extension of the propensity French-Canadians had for large families. But as soon as these children began to grow and to express themselves in society, it quickly became clear that they bore little resemblance to the children and adolescents who preceded them. They were a different breed, who brought rupture and change; they were indeed children of the baby boom.

In other words, even if the purely quantitative aspect of the phenomenon was less prominent in Quebec than elsewhere, the *baby-boom effect* itself was felt at least as strongly. By baby-boom effect I mean that general disturbance of social equilibrium, mental attitudes, lifestyles, and living conditions that the population's suddenly becoming younger and the massive appearance of a new generation on the world stage would favour.

The duration and suddenness of the rise in the birth rate

were more than enough to alter significantly the age pyramid in Quebec, but two other factors combined to reinforce, and in some ways aggravate, the baby-boom effect.

First, there was geography. The baby boom was most prominent in North America, that is, in English Canada and the United States, where it assumed gigantic proportions.* Contrary to what is often believed, Quebec society was not an isolated entity, closed in on itself and more or less immune to what was going on elsewhere, especially in the United States. During the forties and fifties, American influence in Quebec was very much on the increase, due in part to a weaker French influence as a result of the war but primarily to an explosion in new means of communication. Through radio, film, and soon television, as well as travel to Plattsburgh or to the New England coast, Quebeckers were living more and more within the cultural and ideological orbit of the United States. It was as though the border had ceased to exist. And so the upheaval caused by the baby boom within American society could not help but have repercussions on Quebec.

Quebec's case is by no means unique. The United States was then at the height of its political, military, and economic power. Its influence, thanks to its control over the new mass culture, extended throughout the West, if not the entire planet. Whatever change might take place within its borders would immediately reverberate in any country under its sway — in other words, just about everywhere. An American trend, idea, or preoccupation was almost instantly adopted by the whole Western world. That is why the baby-boom

* On this topic, see the extremely informative book by Landon Y. Jones, *Great Expectations: America and the Baby-Boom Generation* (New York: Ballantine Books, 1981).

effect, linked initially to local issues, could not remain local for very long. It quickly became a phenomenon affecting all of civilization, and its impact was felt even in societies where the baby boom did not occur, or where it assumed more modest proportions. Such was the case, notably, in Western Europe. In France, Germany, Italy, and Great Britain the war left scars and created a climate of confusion far removed from the euphoria that reigned in America. In strength and persistence, the rise in the birth rate fell far short of that of the American baby boom. Yet these countries, too, especially from the sixties on, would be shaken by the enormous seismic wave moving across the Western world, courtesy of the baby-boom effect, and made in the U.S.A. In this sense, the conditions that paved the way for the student riots in Paris in May of 1968 had their beginnings in the maternity wards and homes of America at the end of the war.

Is it feasible that Quebec, sitting at the gates of the empire, a stone's throw from the epicentre, could have avoided the impact of the baby boom or have experienced only a watered-down version? Not likely.

In fact, rather than being sheltered from the baby-boom effect, Quebec found itself in a situation that made it more vulnerable than other countries and therefore felt its repercussions all the more deeply. And this vulnerability stemmed, paradoxically, from Quebec's very stability, or at least the appearance of stability that was its hallmark.

While the Quebec that preceded the Quiet Revolution was not, as has often been claimed, a monolithic and reactionary community closed in on itself and utterly resistant to change, its institutions and social life, opinions and customs were characterized, not by stasis exactly, but by a cautious approach to the changes and new ways of living and thinking associated with what we call, with some confusion, modernity. Despite internal and external pressures, this conservative climate managed to survive and hold back the shifts in values and mental attitudes that had occurred in other countries since the turn of the century, especially our southern neighbour. And so Quebec was to a certain extent a kind of enclave where, on the surface at least, the structures and signs of the old order were able to hold their own more successfully than elsewhere.

In the wake of the baby boom, what survived of this bulwark was now nothing more than a fragile source of aggravation. Not only was the old order too weak to resist the desires and the momentum of the new generation — it would melt away, in fact, with a rapidity we would find disturbing even today — but it had sustained itself for so long that matters were only made worse and its downfall was all the more devastating.

While in Western Europe and the United States the baby-boom effect, despite its scope and the seriousness of the changes it provoked, could be viewed as the outgrowth and intensification of a modernizing trend that had existed since much earlier in the century, such an assimilation would be more difficult, if not impossible, in Quebec. Here, given the distinctive history or historical consciousness, the cast of mind and goals of the new generation would have no antecedent; they would have no links with any tradition or any part of the past, but would emerge as an absolute beginning, which could only underline their force and enhance their disruptive nature.

In fact, the pre-Quiet Revolution Quebec, with its backwardness and ideological marginality, represented a kind of privileged environment that was particularly favourable to the full manifestation of the baby-boom effect. As they took their first steps in the world, what better terrain could these *enfants terribles* find than a society hemmed in by the cult of the past and respect for authority, one that was suspicious of change and deferential to profoundly conservative elites, yet blessed at the same time with enough riches to assure it a good standard of living? More than any other environment, Quebec offered this generation everything it needed to pursue fully the revolutionary task it was convinced had been conferred upon it.

For some time now, certain specialists have become accustomed to seeing Quebec society as a kind of laboratory in which it is possible to study *in vivo,* and on a small and therefore manageable scale, grandiose phenomena that otherwise would be impossible to observe and measure correctly. Thus, in the thirties and forties, teams of sociologists from the great American universities visited Quebec to do "field" analyses of traditional rural societies. Later, demographers and geneticists from around the world showed considerable interest in the Quebec population, one of the most homogeneous and best inventoried in the West, a unique sample that would allow them to verify empirically their most general hypotheses. Now, it seems to me it would be worth doing a comparable investigation of the effect of the baby boom on modern civilization. And Quebec is such an exemplary and simple case that it is an obvious choice for a study that would reveal the scope of the baby boom's repercussions and the mechanisms that made them possible.

So Quebec can therefore pride itself on one more claim to fame: as the Promised Land for the baby-boom effect, an environment where the baby boom could fulfil its true potential.

THE BIRTHRIGHT

The lyric generation was only the advance party, the very first wave of the baby boom, but this position gave it a considerable advantage. Thanks to the great numbers of children who came in their wake, the boys and girls of the lyric generation would possess, as the group that represented the whole baby boom, a force that would enable them to stand up to their elders and to profit fully from the demographic shift and its effect on every sphere of social life.

But there was another advantage that distinguished the lyric generation from the generations that preceded and followed it, especially those baby boomers who were born at a time when the lyric generation had already emerged from childhood and had begun to make its way in the world.

Too often, we tend to see the baby boom as a seamless, monolithic phenomenon and to regard all children born during the fifteen or twenty years it lasted as a single, unique "megageneration," as Landon Jones puts it, with the same history and attributes. But such was not the case, for at the heart of the baby boom is a crucial division that separates the older from the younger, especially the lyric generation itself from the multitudes that followed it.

To properly grasp this division, let us look again at the

way the baby boom developed. As customarily defined, it lasted from the end of the Second World War to the beginning of the sixties. But what this global definition does not always state, and what risks being forgotten, is that the birth rate did not increase constantly over these years, nor did it stay at the same level. Rather, the process unfolded in two separate and opposing phases. The first was the explosive phase, during which the birth rate, which had risen abruptly towards the end of the war, continued to grow year after year and peaked around 1957. Then came a second phase in which the rate reversed itself, and while it continued for some time to exceed the norm, it began a gradual decline that would intensify and last right through the sixties, far beyond the so-called age of the baby boom.

In other words, even though the boom resulted in an abnormal increase in the overall number of births, the definition only applies, strictly speaking, to the first, relatively brief phase, since the slowdown began in the second half of the fifties, with a decline in growth and a gradual return to normal.

The lyric generation corresponds only to the first of these two phases. But the true lyric generation was an even narrower group: the oldest of the oldest, that is the very first born, who came into the world between the last years of the war and about 1950.

To my mind, the difference between these two phases is crucial. It implied much more than a simple reversal of demographic trends; it heralded a change in the existential climate, the transition from a certain attitude towards life and vision of the future to a totally different attitude and vision. For if optimism and the certainty of being at the dawn of a new world are what inspired the first, or ardent, phase of the baby boom, then for that movement to tire and begin to reverse itself, to take a negative turn, these feelings must not only have weakened — a normal development for any excitation — but they must have given way to the opposite sensation, a kind of uneasiness or lassitude, perhaps, or at least caution — in any case, a very different approach to life. It is difficult to explain this change and to say what went on in the minds of parents at that time. No doubt the greater accessibility of contraception played a role, although the birth rate had begun to slow before the pill became available. The economic climate could also have had an effect: the almost constant growth since the war stagnated towards the end of the fifties. But it is also possible that the decision henceforth to cut back on births was inspired by the parents' desire to keep themselves free for their firstborn and to respond to their needs without requiring them to grow up or to step aside in favour of younger brothers and sisters. Thus, the weakening of the baby boom would be due to the baby boom acting on itself, or more precisely to the lyric generation acting upon the baby boom of which it was part.

Nevertheless, these two phases — one ascending, the other declining — and the shift in climate that they represent enable us to distinguish between two groups that are usually lumped together as the baby boom: the firstborn, who came into the world during a period of confidence and expansion, and the younger children, who were born into a world whose future appeared less certain or desirable and were not received with the kind of rejoicing that accompanied the arrival of their older siblings. If the former were children of the dawn, the horizon had already begun to darken for the latter. Not only were their destinies to be different, but so were their sense of themselves and their place in society, their aspirations, and their feelings about life.

Even if it had been limited to these circumstances and to

the view of the world they engendered, the advantage bestowed on the lyric generation by its birthright would already have been considerable. But it went much further and was much more *real* than that. Not content to appropriate, thanks to its position, most of the windfalls brought about by an event as dramatic as the baby boom, the lyric generation was able to avoid almost all its negative consequences, which the children who followed had to confront head-on.

Like any abrupt demographic change, the baby boom was a double-edged sword. On the one hand, this eruption of children and young people was a blessing; it created, in a single stroke, a younger population, giving society new ardour and vitality, and forcing it to rethink itself, to change its ways, and to progress. The baby boom certainly had a galvanizing effect on those societies where it occurred, calling into question old practices and provoking or accelerating reforms. In Quebec, for example, the Quiet Revolution might not have taken place, or at least would not have been what it was, if the governing powers and institutions of the day had not been under enormous pressure from a numerous and demanding younger generation.

But there are limits to any society's flexibility, limits beyond which it can no longer adequately respond to the need for change. And that is what happened with the baby boom. After causing such ferment, the massive influx of young people continued and grew in scope, and was finally revealed for what it actually was: a disruption that could no longer be dealt with effectively. The number of young people continued to multiply to the point where society quite simply was no longer able to assimilate them as it had those who had come before. There was a glut. What had been opened closed, and what had been dynamic ground to a halt; there was a kind of blockage. The blessing had become a nightmare.

These two faces of the baby boom, these two moments in its unfolding, were, of course, a blessing for the older, a nightmare for the younger. But the fate of one depended directly on that of the other. It was *because* of the large numbers of younger people and the pressure they put on society that everything opened up for the older group, and it was *because* the older ones preceded them that the younger ones found there was nothing left.

One of the best examples of this dual effect was in the area of employment. When the older baby boomers entered the job market at the end of the sixties and during the seventies, employment was in full growth. Not only did these older baby boomers find work easily and without many qualifications, but they were often able to choose from among a number of positions those that most closely corresponded to their ambitions or personal tastes. Then, once employed and because demand still exceeded supply, they were extremely mobile, quickly moving up the ladder or leaving one job for a more desirable one, and always demanding and obtaining unprecedented working conditions.

But what they did not see, or did not want to see, was that one of the main reasons for this growth, and therefore their prosperity and security, was that behind them was this multitude of children, often their own brothers and sisters, who would require a whole variety of goods and services. This mass would have to be fed, cared for, taught, entertained, managed, given the wherewithal for its purchases and dreams; it was enormous, and there was no limit to its appetite. It formed, in short, a huge market, highly generative, as the economists would say, of employment and profits. Certainly, the first-wave baby boomers were not alone in reaping the benefits, but no one else did so as precociously or as abundantly.

When the younger boomers came knocking on the door
of the job market, conditions had completely changed. There
were no children behind them, for their older brothers and
sisters had few if any. But even more important, there were
no more jobs, nor would there be for a long time, because
their older siblings, who occupied them, had acquired rights
that made them impossible to dislodge, and they were only
thirty or forty years old.

The newcomers could thus knock at the door as much as
they liked, but no one was there to open it for them. Or when
the door did open, it was either to offer them crumbs —
minimum-wage positions, short-term contracts, freelance
work, second-class jobs — or to demand qualifications and
experience that went far beyond what their predecessors —
those making the demands — could boast at their age. Or
even now.

But the contrast between the living conditions for the
firstborn of the baby boom and those of their younger siblings
went further: the two groups entered society under completely different circumstances. From every point of view,
whether social or economic status, prestige or power, resources available to them or expectations in life, the disparity
between the two broad generations of the baby boom — in
particular the alienation of the younger group and its exploitation by the older one — was such that it could be said to
be, if such language were not out of date, a classic dominant
–dominated relationship.

Certainly, the young could protest, rebel, challenge the
system, try to unseat their elders, or demand they be better
treated. And this they did from time to time, in different ways.
But their rebellion was mostly symbolic — when it did not
in fact backfire — and it was unarmed and therefore doomed
in advance. For it lacked numbers, that simple yet essential

resource that had been the weapon of their older siblings, who had relied not only on their own numerical weight, but also on the enormous weight of their juniors; they spoke out and made their demands in the name of the baby boom as a whole. The involuntary solidarity that had linked the young to their older siblings, and from which the latter profited enormously, was not reciprocated, for this time the rebellion was directed against the older siblings themselves.

We can see how history and demography favoured the children of the lyric generation, whose greatest asset was to be born before all the others. They were infinitely better endowed in every way than earlier generations, and their destiny bears no comparison to the fate of those who followed, those who had no choice but to suffer the effects of that same imbalance that had been such a boon to their older brothers and sisters.

CHILDHOOD REINVENTED

The lyric generation's experience with the job market is just one example of the ease with which every phase of its life would unfold. But there is no need to wait for the children of the war and immediate postwar period to reach adulthood to find evidence of that ease. The lucky star that would always light their path had begun to shine much earlier, during their childhood and early adolescence.

When we examine what the world and society were like between the end of the forties and early sixties, when the children of the lyric generation were growing up and dutifully pursuing their education, we are struck by the many factors that contributed to their security and happiness.

First, from an economic point of view, it was the beginning of what Jean Fourastié would call the "thirty glorious years," or what was for the West a period of unparalleled prosperity, marked by a steady rise in the standard of living, an acceleration of technological development, and the rapid expansion of consumerism. For the children of that time it meant a princely childhood, one not only sheltered from need and anxiety, but filled with goods and amenities of all sorts. The lyric generation was the first to experience, from early on, what we might call the normalization of riches.

Another important factor was the change in the very definition of childhood and its position within society.

The end of the forties and all of the fifties represented the quintessential age of the child. From the new, rapidly growing middle class to the poorest of the poor, from the country to the cities, and from the crowded alleyways of town to the shaded avenues of the suburbs, the land was teeming with boisterous, squealing boys and girls with no other care but their games and secret rites, their friendships and group rivalries, their forts and bicycle races. This proliferation, this deafening tide of children, gave the society of that era, and even its economy, its distinctive character.

Primary schools, summer camps, public swimming pools, and other play sites multiplied; Nestlé Quik made its way into every household along with Kellogg's cereals and peanut butter; the publishers of Superman and Tarzan books, encyclopaedias for young people, and the thrilling Hardy Boys and Nancy Drew novels made money hand over fist, as did the manufacturers of Meccano sets, puzzles, and those magnificent rubber dolls that lowered eyelids fringed with long black lashes as soon as they were stretched out on a bed.

During this time, television — which had just appeared on the scene and had become as omnipresent in homes as religious pictures had been in other times — purposefully devoted a large proportion of its resources and its airtime to the imaginary world of children. In doing so, it ensured its own future, since viewers accustomed to seeing themselves mirrored on its screen and to assimilating its tastes and interests would not soon turn their backs on such audiovisual solidarity and the pleasures that went along with it. On the contrary, the more time passed, the more they demanded that the small screen reflect them entirely.

But the prominence of children is only a secondary

aspect — or one of the manifestations — of a basic ideological or anthropological phenomenon. This phenomenon — revolution, in fact — was the emergence, in the discourse and social practice of the time, of a new model, a new way of understanding and dealing with childhood. The myth of the child saviour was already inherent in the appearance of the lyric generation. This myth has existed since the beginning of time. But in the past it was always associated only with the newborn, through whom was perpetuated the miracle of life, seen as the reenactment of the world's beginning and so as a guarantee of the world's survival. Once this first moment had passed and the newborn had become a child, the myth was reapplied to the birth of another being. This was, then, a myth of birth rather than a myth of childhood. One of the characteristics of modern history, associated with the decline in infant mortality and the spread of birth control, would be the "discovery" of childhood and its gradual elevation to the rank it now occupies, that of a unique and exemplary age.

To better grasp this secular revolution, we can draw on the work of Philippe Ariès to identify three stages in the development of childhood. In the first, which lasted to the seventeenth century, childhood barely existed as a social category. Children immediately became part of the community on which they depended for their survival, but they were in no way distinguished by either the circumstances of their life or by custom. As an existential experience, childhood was certainly an identifiable period, but children did not form a society distinct from that of adults. Their games, clothes, joys, and sorrows showed they were one with the world.

In the second phase of this evolution — the recognition of childhood — children were separated from the rest of society and considered a group apart, with their own needs and characteristics. This separation served to better protect

and support the child. But it was also based on the idea —
and this was new — of the fragility and "idiocy" of the child,
that is, its inferiority, and therefore the need for elders to work
for the child's improvement before it could be admitted into
society. "To be a child," said Bossuet, "is to live like a beast."
It was, in short, a time of probation, a waiting period, which
parents and educators had the responsibility of making as rich
as possible. During that period the child remained a different
sort of person, one without a voice, protected yet controlled,
loved yet subservient.

This state of affairs continued till the middle of our
century and was the kind of childhood our parents experienced.

However, a totally different notion of childhood, one
based on the inviolable autonomy and *superiority* of childhood, had been conceived long before — during the time of
Rousseau, in fact. This idea — or myth — which still applies
today, defines childhood as the seat of beauty, vitality, and
pure spontaneity. Although accepted now by all "develop-
mental" psychologists, this deification of childhood was then
confined to theory and literature. In reality, that is, in law and
customs, in everyday attitudes and practice, the old model
continued to prevail. Even though they were lovingly adored,
children were still treated as imperfect beings, precious certainly, but incomplete, and by virtue of that fact obliged to
bend to the authority and strictures of adults. Thus it was that
only fifty years ago, the strap and spanking were considered
perfectly normal disciplinary measures both at home and at
school.

In fact, it is only since the Second World War that the
new myth of childhood succeeded in altering the lives of
families and individuals. Only then did the wholehearted

"liberation" of childhood — the third stage — take hold. This stage could be viewed as the synthesis of the two that preceded it: children came back into society but still constituted a distinct and "autonomous" group. What had changed, in effect, was not so much the distinction between children and adults as the relative positions of these two groups and the way they related to each other. Childhood continued to be a world unto itself, with its own mentality, values, rules, and myths — its own culture, as the sociologists would say. But childhood — and this is what is new — was no longer considered a time of apprenticeship, of incompleteness, a waiting period for the real life of adulthood, as before. Rather, while still remaining distinct from the rest of life, childhood became a life in and of itself, as legitimate and complete, if not more so, as succeeding stages of life. Without sacrificing individuality, without being assimilated by or participating in the community, this childhood kingdom became, within that community, a territory ruled by its own laws and values. It was the adults who now had to conform to those laws and values.

The lyric generation was the first to profit fully from this promotion, or emancipation, of childhood, which distinguishes it, once more, from all previous generations. The lyric generation reinvented childhood. For the first time, children were no longer treated as children, as incomplete beings who needed moulding or as interim foreigners waiting to be admitted to society. And for the first time, childhood represented a social category in its own right, one that was still dependent, certainly, but integrated into the social fabric and able to some degree to impose its standards and its demands on groups other than children themselves.

This new status was to have a lasting influence on the lyric generation's feelings about its place in society. While living in a world apart like all children before them, those of this generation were in no way excluded or marginalized. They could therefore remain themselves and continue to explore their universe, for it was no longer children who conformed to the world, but the world that opened up to children.

THE BLESSINGS OF BEING IN TRANSITION

This situation had its consequences, as we would see in the decades to come. But while the lyric generation was still in its infancy or early adolescence, what it was and what it said made little difference. Life seemed to have changed very little. And despite their respect for their offspring, adults had the upper hand: not only did the responsibility for society fall to them, but they assumed it totally and without question for the good and happiness of their children. These children may not have been like those who preceded them, but the world, for the time being at least, continued to turn much as before.

And therein lies yet another privilege accorded the lyric generation, that of being *in transition*, which again required no effort but was part and parcel of the other gifts history had bestowed on it.

Born and raised in a well-ordered world, these children and young adolescents were able to take advantage of the best and most useful things the world had to offer. Yet the world never really weighed heavily on them or oppressed them. Constraints had become extremely lax, for this old world knew it was in decline and was ready to give way to the new world that would soon rise up to favour the lyric generation.

This reality becomes crystal clear when we look at the education this generation received in Quebec between the beginning of the fifties and the middle of the sixties. From today's perspective, their education appears to be one of the best any generation ever had, which was a direct result of its transitional character, halfway between the old and the new, between tradition and change. The old system was becoming increasingly outmoded, but still retained much of its force, and the new pedagogic thought just beginning to emerge had not yet taken the systematic form it later assumed. These two universes overlapped and complemented each other; each corrected its course in response to the other's moderating influence, so that their respective qualities were reinforced and their faults, if not eliminated, were largely tempered.

Were we to go by external appearances and declared principles alone, the education received by the first-wave baby boomers appeared no different from that received by their parents and by previous generations of French Canadians. The curriculum and texts had hardly changed since the end of the nineteenth century. Religion was still the focus and infiltrated practically every discipline. Teaching methods had not changed much either, nor had the hierarchy of the school system or the relationship between teachers and students, which was predicated on discipline — or if necessary coercion — and respect for authority. And of course, the clergy was present in every facet of children's lives: at home, where its influence was exerted through the parents, and in school, where the clergy often taught and was always in charge.

But beneath this facade of stability, if not total stagnation, important changes were beginning to take place, not so much in the system itself as in the spirit that moved it — the mental attitudes of parents and educators, for adults were becoming more and more affected by the new myth of childhood. These readers of Dr. Spock and his disciples, not to mention Freud and Piaget, were slowly modifying their ideas on how to raise and educate young people. Bearer and harbinger of a new world, the child was no longer regarded as someone to be moulded and "broken," but as the depository of a unique treasure that had to be protected and enhanced. Where in the past peopled regarded children as animals to be tamed or clay to be shaped, they now spoke of children as flowers that had to be nurtured and allowed to blossom without any interference other than lavishing them with air and light and protecting them from possible danger.

It was within the family that the new attitude really took hold. In the past considered just another mouth to feed — thus as an inferior member of the family unit — the child now became prince of the household. The family's whole life and budget were organized with his protection and happiness in mind. Certainly, parents retained their authority, but they exercised it less rigidly and more gently. They tried to get close to their children, allowed themselves to be addressed in familiar fashion, joined in their games, punished them with reluctance, became their pals and their confidants. Of course, they wanted to pass on their values and convictions, too, but they endeavoured to do so less by constraint than by example and persuasion. At the same time, parents' burdens and responsibilities increased. To ensure that their children were sheltered and nourished until they could survive on their own was no longer enough. Now parents felt bound to cultivate the full flowering of their youngsters. In other words, not only to cater to their material needs, but also to know how to talk to them and listen to them, to love them without spoiling them, to be their advisers, guides, and friends, all the while leaving them sufficient leeway and freedom. In short, during this period of transition, parents wanted to provide their children with as much support and as few constraints as possible, to be both intimate and discreet, available and self-effacing.

In the areas of school curricula and teaching methods, change was more gradual, and it would take another ten years before Rousseau's vision of the child finally prevailed. While members of the lyric generation were at their school desks, the new vision of the child was still only an ideal, but its influence was already being felt. Although it was not yet accepted into new pedagogic practices, this vision acted implicitly on existing ones, so that the old system found itself mellowed from within. Administrators and teachers — many of them, at any rate — tried to modify their methods and attitudes, to temper their authority, to be more open to the needs and desires of the students. And the yoke of the past, while not entirely removed, became much lighter than it had been.

Such was the case in Quebec's classical colleges. During the fifties and up to the middle of the sixties, these colleges appeared not to have changed. Run by the clergy and restricted officially to an elite of young people destined for the priesthood or the liberal professions, they offered a traditional, humanist curriculum that lasted eight years, was steeped in religion, and emphasized Latin, Greek, the humanities, and philosophy. These were profoundly conformist institutions of the old order, committed to an authoritarian education and removed from modern life.

However, if we take a closer look at these colleges and what they were when the lyric generation attended them, we cannot help but observe that their principles and traditions, even though still officially adhered to, had become much less binding. The old classical college had endured in form, but was becoming more modern in content.

Many teachers, who now included a large number of laymen, and clergy, who were still in charge of administration, seemed to relinquish their rigidity of earlier days and adopted an attitude of openness, curiosity, and sensitivity to the problems and preoccupations of the students that bore no relation to the "serene possession of the truth," which had been their pride up to then.

This change was reflected first of all in their teaching. Without actually revising the curriculum, educators gradually brought pedagogical methods up to date and even allowed a certain amount of innovation. In Latin and Greek, for example, they introduced the study of ancient customs and civilization, which did not replace traditional lessons in grammar, but supplemented them and brought them to life. In literature, Bossuet, Pascal, and Corneille were still studied, but more time was devoted to the romantics and symbolists, to contemporary authors and French-Canadian literature, and the way in which they were presented was modernized. Officially, the *Index* (list of forbidden books) was still in force, and permission was needed to read Baudelaire or Camus, but any college student could, with or without permission, immerse himself at his leisure in *The Stranger, The Flowers of Evil, Lady Chatterley's Lover,* and many other forbidden books that could be found in paperback at the local bookstore, if not at the college itself. In philosophy, Saint Thomas was simply a pretext for younger teachers to refute — and therefore deal with — a number of less orthodox thinkers; his immortal psychology was confronted with the more complex views of Freud; Aristotle's *Politics* with the excesses of Marx; scholastic realism with the inadequacies of Hegelian idealism or Sartrian existentialism. Even mathematics and the sciences were no longer the poor relations they had been in the past.

At the same time, libraries, laboratories, and gymnasiums

were improved and modernized in almost all colleges. And so were conditions for students. The number of day students was increased; regimentation of boarders was relaxed from year to year; social backgrounds were more varied; and rules and discipline became generally less rigorous. Of course, all students still had to make regular visits to their spiritual adviser, but discussions centred on chastity and vocation soon gave way to conversations about art, theatre, film, or sport. And of course, proper behaviour in class and regulation uniforms were still musts, but the controls rarely went beyond that, and leeway for the individual continued to grow.

The concept of personal fulfilment made inroads and had its effect. Extracurricular activities proliferated, intensified, and became — as it was termed — autonomous. It was the golden age of student newspapers, collaborative poetry collections, and amateur theatre groups, of film clubs, and soon, student unionism and participation.

The classical colleges' reputation for being a closed, quasipenitential world that stifled desire and personality may have been valid in the past, but it no longer corresponded to the experience of the majority who attended such colleges in those years. These colleges were on the contrary animated and lively environments that were in the throes of change and where a kind of restlessness reigned in both the students and their teachers.

It is true that classical schooling was available only to a minority. But this minority, or this elite as it was then called, continued to expand, and the children of workers and humble employees had much easier access to a classical education than had been the case till then. This was a result not only of the rising standard of living and relative stability of educational fees, but also because more and more parents wanted their children to have an education superior to their own. Faced with this growing demand, existing institutions expanded, new ones were founded each year, including several colleges for girls, and schoolboards opened classical sections in their public high schools.

And so, things were on the move, though perhaps not as rapidly as desired. But the evolution was no less real. Without transforming itself radically or abandoning its basic structures, the classical education system of the time divested itself bit by bit of its most flagrant faults: tediousness, glorification of the past, intolerance, and elitism. In that respect, it was well and truly in decline. However, this decline did not deprive it of its most precious qualities: modestly sized institutions, a supportive environment for the students, a broad general education, and a sense of culture. Thanks to this rare and fleeting equilibrium typical of periods of transition, this mix of custom and progress — of order and adventure, as Apollinaire would say — this encounter between a vibrant yet disappearing tradition and an emerging liberalization, the classical colleges knew their finest hour. It was a time when the blessings of decadence linked hands with those of new beginnings.

But this period lasted only ten or fifteen years at the most. With the arrival of further cohorts of the baby boom, with their increased demands, classical education was declared unsalvageable. It was scuttled purely and simply. Such thoughtlessness seems inconceivable today. How is it that this institution was judged solely on the basis of its principles, which were, granted, those of another age, without regard for what it had become in practice or how much it had been transformed? One explanation for this blindness is that the lyric generation sought only to satisfy its craving for rupture and renewal in every domain and at any price.

So the younger members of the baby boom were herded

into comprehensive schools and Cegeps, and the privileged status of their older siblings was once more reinforced. Not only did the lyric generation benefit from the stability of a system whose virtues were well established, but they also profited from the advantages that came with reform, without having to put up with any of the inconveniences or disruption reform brought in its wake. Once again, they were the cosseted children of transition.

The lyric generation was therefore both the last of the old world, whose stability it enjoyed without having to deal with the repression, and the first of the world to come, into which it leapt with all the more gusto given the safety net from the past suspended beneath it.

Part Two

YOUTH

THE GREAT TIDE

Until the sixties, the impact of the lyric generation on society was not felt in any marked way. For the children of the immediate postwar period, the hour of public life had not yet tolled. Surrounded by parental affection and the benevolence of teachers who were respectful of proprieties and tradition, they grew up peacefully in a world that offered them security and fulfilment. No one could foresee the unique fate the future held in store for them. They themselves did not foresee it, for they were not yet aware of their power.

This power was nevertheless already making itself felt. But indirectly, mutely. It had not yet acquired the visibility and the imperative character that it would soon take on, as the lyric generation, emerging from the cocoon of childhood and early adolescence, entered the new age of youth, where it could at last stand up and make its voice clearly heard.

Contemporary history and sociology commonly associate the sixties with the explosion of the "youth movement," which was the rise, all across the West, of a new generation whose disruptive presence shook to their foundations the most firmly established institutions, and whose temper, mores, and expectations provoked the decline or transformation of long-entrenched codes and traditions. A pivotal time that was both strange and miraculous, this decade in retrospect took on epic proportions. Like any epic, it had its great unifying themes (protest and rock), its memorable events (Woodstock and the student protests of May 1968), its legendary heroes (students and hippies), not to mention all those writers, intellectuals, and social scientists who have remained its most devoted and enthusiastic chroniclers. And in fact, seen as a moment of explosive energy, pure freedom, challenge, and affirmation, this period had something about it that was magical.

But it owes its renown mostly to those — and they are many — who turned twenty in the course of those years and who persist today, despite their greying hair, in regarding the decade as a kind of golden age. From the vantage point of their forties, they see in those bygone days the symbol of what is or was best in them, the perfect model for what life ought to be. For never had the lyric generation been so authentically itself as during this brief period, never had it been so assured, so certain of the sweep and legitimacy of its powers, and never had it felt so noble and so innocent. Never, in short, had it been so convinced of being loyal to its manifest destiny or so close to the ideal it had carried within it from birth. So it is natural that in the eyes of those who lived during this time, the memories of the sixties gradually took on the appearance of a founding myth.

However evocative it may be, the term *the sixties* is not quite exact. The period that corresponds to the youth of the lyric generation began during the first half of the sixties and lasted until about the middle of the following decade. That is when the firstborn baby boomers turned twenty and embarked on that phase of their life that was no longer adolescence but not quite adulthood. This was a happy period twice over, for it represented the generation's debut, the first great demonstration of its force and its genius, and it was an incursion as yet unsullied by any responsibility. The moment had finally come to express oneself and test one's faculties in the world, but without having to manage that world, or to assume its weight.

What was genuinely new about this period, then, was the sudden *visibility* of the lyric generation and the space it now began to occupy not only in the material and economic sphere, but in the political, cultural, ideological, and moral world, that is, in the very heart of the community.

Today we often underestimate the degree to which this abrupt emergence of youth, and the rupture it represented, affected not so much the population (whose average age had been dropping since the start of the baby boom, fifteen or twenty years earlier), as society itself, that is, the sector of the population that both defines and complies with the rules and objectives established by and for the community. Given the speed with which it was achieved and the proportions that it took, this breakthrough on the part of youth was a completely unprecedented phenomenon and unlike anything that had transpired in the past between different age groups in society.

Such upheaval was the result of several factors, some of which may be ascribed to the young people themselves, others to the older generations into whose midst they were flung. Among the former, the most significant was number. The impact of the lyric generation's numerical weight, representing as it does a fundamental constant over the years, was confirmed in striking fashion. That the young of that period were able to take centre stage to that extent, with their physical presence, opinions, and needs, and that they did so more successfully than ever as the sixties progressed, was due first of all to the overwhelming proportion of the population they represented.

The lyric generation was already much larger than the age group that immediately preceded it (the children of the Depression). But if we add the cohorts of the baby boom that followed, then the number of people that entered the last years of adolescence and the beginning of adulthood between 1965 and the middle of the next decade becomes enormous. Proportionately, this tide of youth constituted by far the most significant and therefore most visible age group in society.

To this numerical factor we must add another, whose effect directly amplifies that of the first. It concerns what analysts have called the prolongation of youth. To be young in former days was a rather thankless condition, which for this very reason, or more likely for economic reasons, did not last long. With rare exceptions, youth was complete at the age of fifteen or sixteen, if not earlier in rural areas. One of the great innovations of modern times — one that the lyric generation again was the first to experience — was the extension of this period well beyond traditional limits, to around the age of twenty at least, if not later still.

Of course, such a change may be explained initially by the greater emphasis on education, due to a transformed economy that required more qualified workers, but also, of equal importance, to the expectations and ambitions parents had for their children. Parents hoped that their young would continue their studies as long as possible, for their personal fulfilment as well as success in their careers, and were willing to meet the needs of their sons and daughters for much longer than their own parents had done. And so they put off the day when they would see their children spread their wings and fully embrace adulthood. What is more, the very evolution of the baby boom made this phenomenon into a kind of fatality; as the number of young people began to exceed the capacity of the job market to absorb them, they found themselves trapped in a state of dependence and unable to escape their youth.

Whatever the causes, the prolongation of youth would arrest what the law of numbers had wrought. Not only were the young proliferating enormously, but they formed an agglomeration that hardly moved, that had no end, that spread, swelled, added to itself, and in so doing, made itself felt more and more. As a result, a new definition of youth, a new way of living and experiencing the condition of being young, gradually emerged and found acceptance. Instead of seeing youth as a phase or a transitional period one quickly passed through, boys and girls now installed themselves in youth; they remained there for ten, twelve, or fifteen years, and were joined by an uninterrupted stream of newcomers who installed themselves in turn, but dislodged no one.

Thus the burgeoning lyric generation had all the appearances of a veritable invasion. Of course, any society needs to renew itself and is constantly augmented by new arrivals. Young people and immigrants join its ranks, contribute new blood, and ensure the future, as Hannah Arendt would say; in other words, they preserve, enlarge, and modify what preceding generations had worked to build. But when these new arrivals are so numerous and their coming so sudden and prolonged that their integration is compromised, when rather than blending into society and being absorbed by it they form what amounts to another population inside the first, then the world is shaken to its foundations and its equilibrium destroyed from within. From that time on, the world can no longer be renewed, can no longer change and still remain true to itself. The only choice is to vanish, dissolve, and make way for a different world, one that is foreign if not hostile to the first and that the newcomers have brought along with them.

It is just this type of transformation — or cataclysm — that the youth movement represented. Its numbers were so impressive and its youth lasted so long that the young were able to form a solid, resistant, and autonomous universe. But above all, perhaps for the first time in history, this world of young people was no longer a secondary, eccentric planet orbiting on its own; its position was now central. The planet itself had become the hub and driving force of the system, and the system was now in orbit around the planet, that is, around the point of greatest density.

The entire system, all of society, was now organized in terms of youth, which had the power to decree and embody norms, to establish goals and values, to justify and inspire action. There had been an invasion, territory had changed hands, and the former occupants had been displaced by a new group superior in number and vitality, which could now impose its law.

The invaders' natural advantages played a crucial role in their triumph, but for an adequate understanding of the youth movement we must also take into account the invaded, the older generations who were already there when the tide rolled in. For they were most vulnerable, and it is their destiny that was at stake.

One of the interesting features of the sixties and early seventies that is rarely pointed out and yet is truly astonishing was the negligible resistance offered by the older generations to the upheaval(s) generated by the rise of the young, and it is astounding even today to think of how easy a victory it was. Far from having to face down hostile elders or to confront a world with an iron will to endure, the lyric generation waltzed into society through an open door, without any serious obstacles being put in its way, and was received with open arms by the very people it was preparing to supplant.

There was the odd skirmish, of course, and even a few battles. Adults, parents, educators, and established authorities objected from time to time — occasionally with vehemence — to the mentality, habits, or aspirations of the young savages. But such resistance was not only short-lived and marginal; most of the time it was purely symbolic. To see all that as episodes in a war waged against youth by older generations determined, come what may, to defend their territory, would be to misinterpret the true meaning of those years. The young, doubtless, often solicited and cultivated confrontation with their elders; they *wanted* conflict. But war never broke out. From the beginning, the enemy laid down its arms and admitted defeat.

While they appeared to be vast uprisings against the system, the monster rallies and rebellious crusades with which the lyric generation likes to identify its youth were — in fact, could only be — directed against nothing and no one in particular. Instead, they were festivals, demonstrations, indeed, where the young flaunted their existence and their numbers, and the euphoria which that provided them. They saw, as some see in poetry, something pure in rebellion and anger; their rebellion and rage were autoreferential, magical, an acting out, fulfilling a cathartic function and taking a ritualized form ordinarily associated with dance or song.

As for the elders, their apparent passivity was not surprising, for given the circumstances they hardly had any choice. Even if they had wanted to, what good would it have done them to dig in their heels? When a wave engulfs you, it is foolish to try to swim against the current.

In fact, only two strategies were available to them. They could surrender unconditionally, leaving the way clear for the new masters. Or they could make an alliance and join the camp of the young in order to defend their own interests.

Neither solution, in fact, prevailed. Rather there was a marriage of submission and collaboration, both of which ruled out conflict.

But to avoid confrontation with the young was not, for adults at that time, just a calculated tactic. Their attitude might also be explained — as I have tried to show in earlier chapters — by the climate within which the lyric generation had been brought into the world and raised. Since their birth, if not their conception, these young people had represented to their parents a new beginning, hope, the prelude to an entirely new era that would be free of the horrors of the past and infinitely better than anything they themselves had known. How could these same parents not feel that their role now was to fade into the background and be silent, or to do everything they could to make the task easier for their sons and daughters, and pave the way for them without interfering? To rise up against their children, to try to impose on them their own world and laws, would have been to betray the faith they had placed in these darlings of the dawn. They had no other choice, in the end, but to grant them sympathy and admiration.

It would therefore be wrong to interpret the "permissiveness" that characterized parents' relationships with their children at that time as no more than indifference and resignation in the face of the irresistible advance of youth. For, in fact, it was nothing less than reverence, a kind of dumbstruck approval; knowing their sons and daughters were both better prepared and stronger than themselves, parents could do nothing more than give their blessing and cooperate. Having neither the means nor the will to oppose the newcomers, these elders not only left the way clear, but many of them fell into step with the young; they tried to look like their children, see the world as they saw it, adopt their values, their ways of being, even their desires.

In this context, it is easier to understand the nature of the notorious crisis of authority that crept into social and family life. This crisis was often defined as the discrediting of all attempts to impose respect or obedience derived from commitment and conviction, without recourse to overt or latent violence. But if we look at it more closely, as embodied in the new relationship between parents and children, and even between older and younger generations, this crisis corresponded less to a disappearance than to a displacement, a reversal of authority. And while it had changed its location and its agent, this authority continued to function with as much efficiency and restrictiveness as before.

Authority, which had been associated since the beginning of time with age and experience, with parents and the elderly, began to migrate as of the sixties, to the opposite pole. From now on the tender and virginal young — "youth" both as an attribute and a community — would garner prestige and the right to command respect. And as with all authority, this right could not be nor was it questioned. Youth was its own justification, like an axiom that serves as a precondition to thought or action. In and of itself, without any proof being necessary, youth constituted a value, a basis for judgements and decisions whose legitimacy or validity could not be disputed. Thus, it was self-evident that youth would prevail over age, that the young were the primary trustees of truth, and that a youthful society oriented towards the future was preferable to an aging society. Just as in times past, despite their weakness and their dependent state, the old people dominated the community by virtue alone of the respect that was accorded them, so the young of the sixties did not have to prove themselves. They had only to be there and to speak; the fate of the world was in their hands.

And so the world, literally, did change hands. It entered a new age, under new control, one that would impinge on all of life in society, if not life itself. For as it disseminated its ideas, feelings, and needs, youth would also impose them on the entire community, which would itself then become young — an immense, all-embracing youth.

THE QUIET REVOLUTION
OR THE REVENGE OF THE
FRUSTRATED REFORMERS

Among the older generations that welcomed this tide of youth with open arms, one group in particular played a crucial role. This was the group made up of what I would call, without any pejorative connotation, the frustrated reformers. Many of them, of course, were parents, but it is a different side to their "psychology" that concerns me here. Others belonged to the Depression generation, which immediately preceded the lyric generation. In many respects, the latter are the more interesting.

To get a good picture of the scenario I am about to describe, in which the characters are groups rather than individuals, it would be best to set the action on a specific stage: that of Quebec.

The period is the Quiet Revolution, a turbulent time characterized by the criticism and rejection of an entire past judged obscurantist and alienating, and by an unprecedented zeal for modernization and innovation. From a political, ideological, and cultural point of view, these years represented a rupture of major proportions. In the minds of its citizens, if not in fact, it was as though the history of Quebec was instantly split in two, and over an old world, exhausted from having endured so long, there suddenly arose a new, modern, miraculous one bursting with freshness and energy. From the corridors of power to the metaphors in poem and song, a new wind was blowing, a wind of genesis and of the founding of a new land. It was the dawn of the world.

Naturally, the arrival of the lyric generation and the spreading of the baby boom, and with it the new ascendancy of youth, were key factors without which neither this climate nor these achievements could have seen the light of day. That said, it was not in fact the young who made the Quiet Revolution happen. In reality, the agents of this rupture, those who conceived, planned, and organized it, were the elders, who had already left youth behind, or were just beginning to do so.

These were the frustrated reformers. Born during the twenties and thirties, they had been reformers, reformists in fact, since the Second World War and increasingly so in the fifties. Many of them identified themselves with the denunciations of the *Refus global* manifesto of 1948, the analyses of the magazine *Cité libre,* the actions undertaken by labour unions, or the opinions of organizations committed to social and intellectual struggle. Their ideas, poems, protests, and appeals for change had created, in the Quebec of Duplessis, if not an organized movement, at the very least some ferment, a milieu in which the rallying cries and passions that would spark the revolution to come were being forged in the guise of theories and hopes.

But at the time nothing around them seemed to budge. They could describe the ideal world as much as they wanted, but the one in which they lived remained dishearteningly old and stagnant. They were a bit like the hero of Buzzati's *The Tartar Steppe*, scanning the horizon, making scrupulous plans for battle, but seeing nothing approaching. Hence the feeling of frustration I attribute to them. While they dreamed of radical change and were prepared to bring it about, these new elites, this "changing of the guard," as historians would soon call them, were powerless against a society that was still firmly in the hands of a conservative political and religious establishment that was frozen with fear of change. In their view, everything was at an impasse, and many chose to make their lives elsewhere, in more favourable intellectual climates.

However, the upheaval generated by the lyric generation as it reached adolescence and youth offered these frustrated reformers an unexpected historical opportunity to take action and have their revenge at last. The traditional elites were overwhelmed by this onslaught of the young with their unbridled freedom and extravagant demands, and the structures securing their authority crumbled completely, exposing their inadequacy and their fragility. By virtue of their existence, numbers, and energy alone, the young had dealt a death blow to the old social order and doomed the regime. Change was now inevitable.

It is to the great credit of this generation of reformers, as well as a good indication of their zeal, that they were resourceful enough to take advantage of this opening and immediately go on the offensive. Capitalizing on the demographic ferment and its destabilizing effects, they were able to establish themselves as the group best qualified to deal effectively with the new circumstances, and to impose their program for change as the necessary and logical solution for the problems of the time. This program, of course, was the Quiet Revolution.

This revolution was not, therefore, the work of the lyric generation itself, nor a simple and direct offshoot of the youth movement. Let us not forget that at the time of the 1960 and 1962 elections, the events that marked the beginning of the Quiet Revolution, the young were not yet old enough to vote. It was the older generation who were the mediators, who took the considerable needs and energies contained in this movement and put them to work, who assumed responsibility for change and engineered it, and who became, as a result, those who shaped a new mentality and designed a now feasible revolution. On their own these reformers could have achieved nothing, or very little, just as they had been unsuccessful up to that point. The young flooding into society gave them the strength they had been lacking.

The most interesting frustrated reformers were those born during the thirties, between the lyric generation and their parents. As they reached their twenties, these sons and daughters of the Depression had been more sensitive than most to the moral and ideological winds of postwar renewal, so much so that the intractable climate of Duplessis' Quebec weighed on them more than on others, and was that much more intolerable to them. They were, therefore, the most impatient of the reformers. But they were in a sense also, ironically, the weakest because since they were born during the lean years of the Depression when the birth rate was at its lowest, there were few of them. And so, after 1960 they would be the most receptive to the rise of the young; they would welcome them as veritable saviours, would see them as the reinforcements who would enable them to make themselves heard and occupy territory that for so long had been inaccessible to them. Roland Giguère, in his 1966 poem "The Power of Darkness," wrote:

> In the dark of life
> it's the light invades
> to besiege the gloom
> and we hail the invader
> for the invader shines
> where the night's obscure
> like a breath of hope
> at the geode's core

So an immediate complicity was established between those who were entering their thirties and the lyric generation itself. The former were like big brothers and sisters to the latter, taking them under their wing, helping them to get to know themselves and voice their demands, supporting their undertakings, endorsing their outbursts as well as their enthusiasms. For a good ten years there would be a total meeting of minds — and interests. These elders, already members in good standing of the adult world annd having a good deal of power in society, were the lyric generation's protectors, familiars, and sponsors, as well as the instrument of their authority. In return, the lyric generation provided those who came just before them with the weight that would fully legitimize them, and a power base vis-à-vis other groups that controlled Quebec society.

We can find excellent examples of this partnership in the political and ideological life of the time. We need only note the rise of the Rassemblement pour l'indépendance nationale (an early separatist party), whose orators, in their thirties, harangued crowds made up largely of students; the success of the "critical" social sciences, practised and taught by former students of Father Lévesque who had been forced into "exile" during the fifties, but were now being actively recruited by universities, which had to expand to deal with the sudden leap in their enrolment; or even the modernization and phenomenal growth of the state and the civil service, due largely to the influx of young people, and requiring the services of the Depression generation.

My favourite example is that of literature, although one could just as easily cite the visual arts or music. The sixties was an exceptional period for Quebec literature. Indeed it was almost miraculous, given the fervour and intensity that characterized it compared with the listlessness of earlier periods. Publishing houses, magazines, and written works of all kinds burgeoned, and their influence spread throughout society. Form and content were modernized, old taboos melted away, outmoded timid provincialism gave way to audacity, innovation, and sudden change. Like the rest of society, Quebec literature underwent a kind of instant rejuvenation that took the form of a vast impulse to redefine everything and begin all over again. For literature, too, it was the dawn of the world.

Analyze the unfolding of this renaissance a little more closely, though, and it is striking that it was not the work of the postwar generation, but rather that of those who came into the world during the Depression and who, at the beginning of the sixties, were in their thirties or even older. With few exceptions, the great works — the landmark achievements that best summed up the times and shed light on them — that set the tone for the "new" Quebec literature and embodied it most conspicuously were produced by authors who had begun to write during the fifties or even earlier, but who up to that point had done so in almost complete obscurity and solitude.

That is particularly true of essays like *The Impertinences of Brother Anonymous* (Jean-Paul Desbiens) and other, more important books, such as *La Ligne du risque* (Pierre Vadeboncoeur), *Une littérature qui se fait* (Gilles Marcotte), or *L'Homme d'ici* (Ernest Gagnon), all published at the beginning of the sixties, but written and conceived, for the most part, in the course of the previous decade.

In poetry the situation was even more striking; *L'Âge de la parole* (*The Age of the Word*), Roland Giguère's landmark volume, often associated with the sixties, was conceived and set down on paper between 1945 and 1960.

Finally, where the novel and theatre are concerned, the most influential and innovative writers were also members of the older generation. So true is this that when we speak of the Quebec literature of that time, it would be more accurate to see it as a discovery rather than an invention, that is, as the emergence of a body of work already extant, but having led a largely clandestine existence.

Of course, the role of the lyric generation was in no way negligible. But it was still a passive role. Certainly, this generation did provide some writers and works that were important to the literary renewal: Marie-Claire Blais, Réjean Ducharme, André Major, and most of the team that produced *Parti pris* were indeed born during the war. But these authors were among the very first members of the lyric generation and did not therefore represent it in all its full-blown glory. Their contribution, however impressive it may be, does not alter the fact that the primary literary role of the youth of the sixties was not to create but to keep abreast of what was written and to read; in short, to be a good public.

This role was crucial for at least two reasons. First, without this mass of adolescents and young adults who began to read and study Quebec literature, to buy books, to admire the writers, to see themselves reflected in their work and ideas, it is certain that this literature would not have known the fervour that it did. And second, the role of the public is not limited to the reading and appreciation of literary works. The public is more than just a target, more than just a clientele; it is also the raw material, the source of inspiration, the milieu from which literature draws, if not its content, at the very least its language, tone, colour, and flavour. Whether an author lives in a time or a milieu that is tranquil or effervescent, stable or subject to change, is important. Quebec writers of the sixties found themselves surrounded and swept along by a society in which a deluge of young people encouraged an enormous upheaval in ideas and values and a kind of over-heating of social life. This fact, there can be no doubt, counted for much in the originality and daring of their work, and therefore in the literary excitement of those years.

The example of Quebec literature seems so interesting because it is easy to generalize from it. Literature helps grasp the position and the role of the lyric generation within the Quiet Revolution as a whole, not to mention the parallel revolutions taking place at the same time in other societies.

It shows again that the coming of the young need not be seen as a trauma pitting the newly arrived against an older generation bound and determined to defend its territory and to avoid or curb the changes brought about by the crumbling of the demographic order. There was not, indeed could not have been and did not have to be, a youth *putsch* in order to dislodge the elders and assume power. In fact, the need to remake society, the plans for reform, the call for radical political, social, and ideological change — all themes of the Quiet Revolution — had already been in the wind for some time, without, however, any likelihood of their being realized in any significant way.

The primary role of the lyric generation and the baby boom was, through their blatant, unavoidable visibility, to transform completely the foundations of the old order, which were now obsolete and irrelevant, and so to make change both possible and inevitable.

The youth of the sixties, in other words, did not have to act. Others did so in their place and in their name. They just had to be there as a rising tide. The Quiet Revolution, when all is said and done, was the older generation embracing this tide and putting it to work so that they might succeed in their endeavours, where in the past they had only failed.

THE CHORUS

> The stage with its action
> was originally conceived as pure vision
> and the only reality was the chorus,
> who created that vision out of itself
> and proclaimed it through the medium
> of dance, music, and the spoken word.
>
> Nietzsche
> *The Birth of Tragedy*

That the Quiet Revolution was the work of the children of the Depression and not that of the lyric generation itself does not mean that the latter did not profit from it. On the contrary, I would even say that one of the essential roles of youth during the sixties, in addition to making change possible and providing its rationale without having to bring it about, was precisely to reap its benefits. This shows once more just how central the lyric generation was.

It was primarily for the young that reforms were introduced. It was with them in mind, and to satisfy their needs and their demands, that society rethought and transformed

itself. Didn't the Quiet Revolution's commitment to modernization and to catching up reflect a desire for widespread
institutional *rejuvenation,* that is, an accommodation — or
subjection — of society to the genius, expectations, and
sovereignty of youth?

It is not surprising that the young should be the primary
if not the only beneficiaries. Let's examine three examples.

First, this period was the great decade of education. It was
in that domain, with the introduction of programs, structures, and educational equipment earmarked for the influx of
young people, that the most spectacular reforms took place
and the most money was spent. The new "State of Quebec"
at that time was above all an enormous agency of educational
services, a conduit through which a large part of the
community's material and intellectual resources was chan-
nelled, as a priority, to the young. First they were provided
with free secondary schooling, then, as they came to require
it, free education at the college level, and finally a moderately
priced university education, with scholarships and grants.

At the same time, the liberal pedagogical theories that had
made a timid appearance during the fifties were standardized
and gained wide acceptance. They soon gave rise to a sweeping
modernization of programs and curricula, designed to strip
away all abstract, authoritarian, and alienating tendencies so
they would conform to the tastes of the students and be
compatible with their lifestyles and personal development, in
short, be agreeable and undemanding.

These innovations would benefit, above all, the younger
members of the baby boom. As for the lyric generation,
educational reform would affect them even more directly, for
it would give them access to a host of employment opportunities as teachers, administrators, and educational consul-
tants, especially at the secondary, college, and university

levels. These jobs not only provided them with good salaries and virtually complete security, but also with considerable freedom of speech and action and the opportunity to devote themselves generously to their own activities and personal development. Nor should we underestimate the social status and real power that was inherent — then — in the noble calling of educator.

These new openings in the field of education were only one byproduct of the groundswell of opportunities conferred on the young of the lyric generation. Another lay in the great work of the Quiet Revolution: the modernization of the state. There, too, recruitment was intense, and the preferred candidates were those trained in the new disciplines of the social sciences and social engineering, in other words, young university graduates. And there, too, since managerial supervision was light and production goals difficult to define, the work was as "human" and unalienating as one could wish. And when on occasion work did dominate the life and thoughts of those concerned, at least they felt they were directly involved in rebuilding the world, in emancipating a people, in making history.

My last example is equally striking: the new status of youth in the economic system. Mass consumption had gained momentum since the war, entering a new era of expansion in the sixties and picking up speed in the decades to come. Thanks to prosperity, goods unavailable up till then or considered superfluous became commonplace, and their consumption was viewed increasingly as an autonomous activity bearing no relation to — in fact as more important than — production. In addition to making this "massification" of the marketplace possible, youth was the first to profit from it, and did so more ardently and abundantly than anyone else, even though its own contribution to production was at best marginal.

Adolescents and young people have always consumed more than they produced, but their consumption, as a consequence, remained limited and virtually restricted to essential goods alone. But the lyric generation had the resources and the desires, and felt itself entitled to partake of these new treasures, which were designed for it expressly anyway. Records, shows, transistor radios, casual clothes, sports cars — an entire market catering to the Pepsi Generation was created, inspired by their tastes and sensibility, and imposed on all consumers, whatever their age or socioeconomic status. The young became the royalty of fashion. Priests wore blue jeans, politicians sported T-shirts, the middle-aged wore their hair like the Beatles. The adolescent look set the standard for good living and a presentable appearance, and adolescent desires represented the norm for merchants and advertisers. The authority of youth exerted itself with ease.

But such benefits, real as they were, were nothing compared to the general retooling of society and all that it represented for young people, in particular, the lyric generation. This reorganization constituted the basic program and the ultimate significance of the Quiet Revolution. But the Quiet Revolution was only a local manifestation of a much more general crisis that affected all the industrialized nations at the same time. This crisis, or transition, took different forms and obeyed different rules depending on the context, whether it was the Fifth Republic in France, Willy Brandt's West Germany, Lyndon Johnson's "Great Society," Dubcek's "Prague Spring" in Czechoslovakia, or the "Trudeau Era" in Canada. Everywhere the times were changing. There was reform, and so there was unrest. And this unrest was created in the name of youth, and relied on it. The story of these years, both from a political and ideological point of view, was essentially that of a civilization once ruled by tradition and the perpetuation of old ways being transformed into an open, mobile civilization, drunk on freedom and change. In other words, a world frankly resistant to youth, which it viewed as an agent of rupture and innovation, gave way to another world that, in a fever of nonstop creation and experimentation, now wanted to give this same youth free rein to express itself and flaunt its desires.

Just as the fifties had opened its arms to children by responding quickly to their needs, so the period from about 1960 to 1975 was a time when the empire of the young extended to cover the world. The community did not try to restrain the young or absorb them, but surrendered to them entirely and took their aspirations and dissent, their impatience and thirst for freedom, and made them their own.

That is why, when I try to get an overall picture of the role of youth in the history of those years and especially in the unfolding of the Quiet Revolution, the image that most readily comes to mind derives from ancient theatre. It is the image of the chorus, an entity that is both plural and unanimous, all voice and no gesture, passive and yet omnipresent, remote from the action and yet its driving force, its very cause.

In the tumultuous scenario of this time, the true protagonist would not be the lyric generation itself. Not for it the heroic acts, the decisive blows, the making of history. Its role, rather, would be to support, accompany, resonate. Not to act, but to observe the action, justify it by its presence and its clamour, and at the end of the road reap the benefits.

But we would be making a mistake to consider the chorus as a purely marginal or external factor. For while it keeps to itself at the back of the stage without intervening or putting its life on the line, while it is safe from reversals of fortune and is only a sounding board for the triumphs and tribulations of the hero, it is always the chorus that pulls the strings and determines the outcome of the story. The protagonists not only act *before* it. Whether they live or die, whether they move heaven and earth and take up arms against men or gods, they do so *for* the chorus, indeed, thanks to it. And they do so within the limits and through the strength it alone provides, according to the rules and in harmony with the ends it alone dictates; its voice, punctuating the action, is but the constant, obsessive reminder of those ends. The heroes, in fact, are not the masters of the chorus, but its emissaries and captives.

As well, we should not be deceived by the apparent passivity of the chorus. It is a transcendental passivity in that in the chorus's mass and single-mindedness there reside the source, the meaning, and the ultimate outcome of all the action. It has no need to act on its own behalf; it has only to be present, to make itself felt and heard. Its passivity is but a sign of its all-powerfulness and invulnerability; it is an attitude that radiates dominion.

THE LIGHTNESS OF THE WORLD

I would like to forego the detached point of view of the historian and take a closer look at this unique character that was the chorus during the dozen years corresponding to the youth of the lyric generation. I want to reenter it and try to grasp what its responses were, whether it was aware of its role and what it meant.

In less allegorical terms, I would like to ask what sort of apprenticeship those ten years represented for the young people who were then coming into the world. What traces did these years leave on their consciousness? How was the lyric generation affected by the view they then forged of themselves and their surroundings?

To answer these questions, I will consider three broad themes that sum up what is central to the cast of mind that has come down to us from that time. These themes, which are also ideas and feelings, have become so familiar to us today and govern our attitudes and our lives to such an extent that we can hardly perceive anymore how new they were then and how violently they broke with the past. The first of these themes, or qualities, is a sense of the lightness of the world.

For countless generations of young people, adult society — that world already there and fully formed before they arrived, the world they found when they crossed its threshold — was like a wall: it rose up before them yet protected them, and always remained securely in place. It represented order, a hard and steadfast reality, permanence. One could rebel against this order, want to change what was there, and try to breach, vault, or push it aside, and sometimes even succeed, but never without having first met it head-on, encountered its resistance, and recognized the need to come to terms with it.

This is because the world, then, was heavy. Although created by man, in some ways it resembled nature. Its function, in response to actions and desires of men, was to create obstacles, to fight for its own survival and integrity, and only to budge, or bend, if at all, ever so slightly and with infinite slowness. Time marched forward on the tips of its toes. Revolutions, crises, and rapid changes of regime occurred only rarely, and when they did, seldom lasted long or disturbed the stability of the world. As Hannah Arendt reminds us, the pace of progress was so slow, so much slower than that of the life and death of individuals, that it was almost imperceptible, and the world, in terms of human existence, seemed unchanging. The world did not alter; it was eternal.

If it was true for adults and old people, it was even more so for the young, whose status as newcomers obliged them not only to remain submissive and powerless, but forced on them an allegiance to a world that welcomed them on the condition that they agree to work for its continuation. Youth, in such a context, was a state of probation; it was inferior and provisional. The young protested and rebelled, but soon admitted defeat, for the world, by definition, remained unmoved and got the better of any challenge.

In the sixties, the world the young saw before them was largely bereft of this bygone immobility. On the contrary, it was a world in motion, prey to changes so deep and wide-spread, so blithely divorced from the past, that it seemed suddenly weightless and evanescent. This world did not try to perpetuate itself or offer resistance to those who wanted to destroy it, but completely surrendered to the upheavals and challenges that assailed it from all sides. With the consent and support of those who ought to have been its defenders, the wall crumbled stone by stone; then it vanished completely, and nothing remained to block the view or inhibit desire. An immense playing field ready for any adventure, the world no longer stood for what was and had been for all eternity, but for what would be, or rather, what was not yet but was on its way. The old world, the already there, had no more substance and seemed to have melted away. The world had become totally weightless at last, and it was this feeling that gave the period its unique air of exaltation.

But for the young at that time such indeterminacy and instability did not appear to be a radical innovation. For them, it was the normal state of affairs. Set down in an era when everything was fluid and in a state of flux, how could they not conclude that the world was utterly light and insubstantial? Everything that existed, that embodied order, and that claimed to be permanent was to them temporary, and there to be criticized, reformed, and surpassed.

No one experienced or expressed this feeling as forcefully as did the lyric generation, the generation of transition. Its position at the very junction of the old and new regimes made it acutely aware of the fragility of institutions and the im-permanence of the world it saw before it. Arriving at a time when society had agreed to become the instrument of con-stant demolition and reconstruction, this generation had for a short time at least known that earlier age when tradition and the will to endure were important, and had seen this "heavy" age come to an end with virtually no resistance. It saw the world that preceded this transformation and that seemed so ordered, stable, and certain of its own immutability, collapse like a house of cards and give way, from one day to the next, to another world with which it had nothing in common. Having witnessed such metamorphosis so early in life, these young people would have come away with the idea that nothing lasts or is made to last. Even the oldest and most unyielding order had no intrinsic right to perpetuate itself; on the contrary, it could be and had to be destroyed and replaced, again and again if necessary. The world could never impose limits to which one would have to adapt, resign oneself, or deal with as best one could in order to survive. On the contrary, it was something malleable that could be toppled almost at will, and its first rule was that it would in turn collapse as other worlds arrived — worlds that were ever lighter and more supple, and ever more in tune with human desires and behaviour.

This sense of the lightness of the world played a crucial role in the psychology of the lyric generation. This inner conviction represented for the young men and women of this generation what the *mal du siècle* represented for young Europeans around 1810, or what *decadence* meant for those of the same age around 1890, or closer to home, what the cult of the absurd signified for a youth that had been marked by the Depression and the war. Conscious or not, explicit or not, this conviction was for them a kind of axiom, or instinct, housed in the most secret reaches of their minds and sensibilities. It controlled the way they looked at life and determined their strategy for living. And it was one of the wellsprings of their solidarity; this was the prime factor that united them and not only linked them with one another, but distinguished them from earlier generations.

The lyric generation could truly be called the "generation of the lightness of the world."

The *mal du siècle,* the decadent spirit, the taste for the absurd, however, were the property of small groups of young people dissatisfied with or cut off from their society. Their state of mind reflected the rejection they felt and their repudiation of the injunctions and decrees of their elders, whom they regarded as "bourgeois" or worse. What was expressed by a Chatterton, Nelligan, or Meursault — and what ultimately shortened the lives of such heroes — was not only their incompatibility with the world already there, but their powerlessness to change anything at all, and their isolation as a result, which made them pariahs in the eyes of their contemporaries.

Such was not the case where the lyric generation was concerned. They saw the world as devoid of weight, as infinitely open and free, at a time when society was asking nothing less than to mutate, to become light, and to reject the burden of the past, and they did not exactly find themselves in exile, banished or scorned by those with power and authority. On the contrary. The sense of lightness that defined the lyric generation did not alienate it or isolate it from other groups, but expressed so purely and so archetypically what society felt that it gave youth the feeling that they were at the centre of the world and on the cutting edge of history, and, therefore, that youth more than any other group represented the spirit, the very resonance of the age. Chatterton's suicide and Nelligan's exile were part of the past.

This difference is reflected in the emotional shadings of each of the sensibilities under discussion. Romantic "melancholy," the "spleen" of the dandies at the end of the nineteenth century, even the "nausea" that attracted the young habitués of the "caves" in Saint-Germain-des-Prés were all permeated with suffering and "ennui." These were thoroughly negative feelings, inspired by the sense that something was lacking, by a vague, all-encompassing lassitude that led them to conclude that where life and the world were concerned there was nothing to be done, and the sooner out of it all, the better. Their expressions and thoughts reflected a kind of passivity, or moroseness, which took the form now of sadness, now of indifference or disgust, but always of a sort of woeful resignation and a decline in the level of vitality.

For the lyric generation things were just the opposite. Their feeling that the world was light made them experience fullness and joy at every moment. Their exaltation was founded not on deprivation but on excess, not on weariness but on an inexhaustible, all-powerful fund of vigour and energy. With a perfectly clear horizon in front of them, individuals felt the freedom to do and become whatever they desired; there was no boundary to the territory placed at their disposal and no limit to their "will to live all sensations, all experiences, all possibilities," as Raoul Vaneigem proclaimed in his 1967 *A Treatise on How to Live for the Use of Young Generations,* which remains one of the best expressions — because it is one of the most dithyrambic — of this new sensibility.

A comparable emotional climate might be found — although on a much reduced scale, since it only applied to a small group of individuals — in the early days of surrealism, just after the First World War. There was something of the special fervour I am trying to describe in the feeling shared by the young poets and artists who founded that movement: the conviction that because the old world and the old reality had lost all their force and credibility, another reality — a sur-reality — had now become accessible and was waiting to be discovered and shaped by the dreams of those young people who felt accountable to nothing and no one, and who saw no limits to their own power. Perhaps nothing better expresses the extreme idealism and optimism that inspired the lyric generation's sense of the lightness of the world than certain ardent passages from the first *Surrealist Manifesto* or the end of *Nadja*. Here we find the same enthusiasm, the same assurance, the same sense of things beginning, the same joy of knowing one is free of all bonds, responsibility, or any weight that would hold one back from taking flight towards the "starred castle" where all possibilities are at one's beck and call, all needs are satisfied and all pleasures can be indulged in without hindrance.

Perhaps that explains the immense popularity the surrealist movement would have among the young artists and writers of the lyric generation. For them "psychic automatism" and the daring exploration of the "real functioning of thought" would become common currency and the self-evident criteria for any work of art, to the point where art degenerated into techniques of improvisation, of "collective creation," and the cult of spontaneity. In more general terms, this affinity doubtless facilitated the absorption of surrealism into advertising, fashion, and current popular culture. After decades of being more or less marginal, the "scandal" of surrealism became, for a whole generation, one of the most faithful reflections of its shared sensibility and the standard for the way it looked at life and the world.

During the sixties and seventies, however, it was not in art and literature that this feeling of the lightness of the world found its outlet of choice, but rather in that most democratic form of expression: popular music. As we know, "pop" music experienced an unprecedented boom, thanks to the growing importance of youth, which had always been its primary audience anyway, and to technological innovation (33 and 45

RPM records, transistor radios, cassette players, and so on). But its form and content changed completely with the advent of *rock,* which would be the sound both of the times and of the new young generation that would dominate it.

Before rock, the standard form of both American and European commercial popular music was the ballad, such as those sung by Bing Crosby. This music was characterized by its slow tempo, and sweet, melancholic lyrics steeped in nostalgia or the pain of love.

This vogue lasted through the fifties and even a little longer. It coincided for a time with that of the *chansonniers* such as Jacques Brel, Georges Brassens, and Léo Ferré, soon to be followed in Quebec by Claude Léveillé, Gilles Vigneault, and Jean-Pierre Ferland. For the first time, perhaps, a youth culture sprang up in response to this openly committed, even militant music, in which the words were of primary importance. The principal if not sole audience for these songs of "substance" were boys and girls under twenty years old, who saw themselves reflected in them, and so were able to set themselves apart from the adult public, who were still loyal to the innocent ditties of yore.

Despite its intensity, the golden age of the *chansonniers* and the acoustic guitar did not last long. Another music, another sound, was unleashed on the world, sweeping aside everything in its path. Rock music bound together an entire generation of young people, unified them, stirred them, expressed their desires and view of the world.

In contrast to the old romantic ballads and "literary" songs imbued with images and ideas of some depth, rock was in perfect sync with the mentality of the rising young, for whom it resonated as an enormous cry of liberation and joy. First exemplified by Elvis Presley, then by a multitude of others, it reached its peak in the second half of the sixties and early seventies, with the British and American rock groups, and such legendary stars as Janis Joplin and Jimi Hendrix. Through it, its listeners knew pure excitement and unadulterated pleasure, with no particular focus other than the sensation of finding themselves in a totally open world, emptied of any history, that they could freely fill with movement and noise. One of its key features was the intensity of the sound level; the volume had to be loud enough to penetrate everything, overwhelm all, make its presence felt as far afield as possible, across the universe if need be, because the universe, where this music was concerned, was but a vast resonator to be saturated with sound waves. The more decibels the better.

It is no surprise that another characteristic of rock was that lyrics disappeared, or at least became less important than the beat, whose insistent repetition drowned the words in an avalanche of pure, indeterminate sound, of clamour and cacophony. This beat was almost always the same: it began softly and became louder and louder, faster and faster, until it reached a climax of excitation and noise (sometimes an extremely high-pitched voice, sometimes a drum solo), after which it would subside, only to repeat the same process again from the beginning. From sequence to sequence, from one acoustic "orgasm" to another, the "song" could continue indefinitely, were it not for the time constraints imposed by radio, or perhaps the exhaustion of the musicians.

Rock was not primarily, as certain ideologues who made it their specialty were quick to claim, an expression of anger or of youthful protest against the social system. Had that been the case, it would not have been admired and embraced so easily by the system itself. Juvenile and lyrical, rock was characterized by its hypnotic, intoxicating effect on listeners, who were bound by no restraints and restricted by no limits,

who danced for joy before the vastness of their own power
and beauty. Rock was the music of the lightness of the world.

* * *

The awareness of finding oneself in a weightless world,
the idea that no reality is final or entirely legitimate, could
influence the life and thought of an individual in ways quite
different from those I have described. In fact, there are *two*
possible reactions to the lightness of the world, with very
different consequences.

The first is a *negative* feeling, the nature of which can be
either tragic or ironic, satanic. For someone who requires
stable reference points, no longer being able to find them
results in insecurity or disorientation; that person feels abandoned, lost, and even, if this desertion becomes unbearable,
subject to despair. The lightness of the world then becomes a
function of its absurdity. This same feeling can also take the
form of a kind of skeptical resignation: if reality is without
substance, then I am but a shadow; nothing has any importance, and everything that considers itself important is only
laughable. It is much better, then, to do nothing, to withdraw
and poke fun at myself.

In fact, these demoralizing feelings inspired by the lightness of the world seem more plausible — and are doubtless
encountered more frequently in history — than their *positive*
counterpart, the delirious exaltation of the young of the sixties
and the beginning of the seventies. But in their case it was
accompanied by, was at once the source of and the precondition for, another feeling that was just as crucial: a sense of their
power and self-worth. If the world seemed so light to them
and if, rather than plunging them into despair, this lightness
excited them to the point where they were filled with joy, it
is because they knew they were capable of taking on the world

and imposing their rule on it, and that they were totally justified in doing so. The lightness of their world did not mean it was escaping them, but that it was offering itself up to them so that it belonged to them absolutely. This kind of property right, this sway that the lyric generation was convinced it held over the world, was and has remained a cornerstone of its psychology.

All this may seem paradoxical if we remember what I said about the special role played by the young in the turbulent history of the sixties: spectators rather than actors, they were onlookers more than participants during the upheavals of this period, grouped about the instigators of change like the chorus around the protagonists engaged in the action. But this role was much less passive than it seems at first glance. It was the principal role, on which everything else depended.

We can see immediately what lessons the lyric generation would learn from such favourable circumstances. Having both inspired and profited from the action, they could, without in any way feeling obliged to act, at least for the moment, believe they were nevertheless at the heart of the action, whose purpose and meaning coincided to all intents and purposes with their own aims and desires. Thanks to the lyric generation's status as both the instigator and recipient of social change, it saw itself, from the very moment it arrived to take its place in history, as being invested with a power it had neither to win or even to claim, since it was bestowed in the normal course of events, again because of its numbers and the devotion its elders afforded it. Thus, from this moment on, and for a long time to come, this cohort saw itself as the centre of the social universe and the legitimate repository of meaning and power, through which all passed and around which all fell into place, as though it had to be so, as though it was self-evident, and there was no need to justify in any way such a privileged status. Society, the state, the world were made for the members of this generation right from the start, and were theirs to own.

To this feeling of "centrality" was added, both as corollary and complement, an absolute confidence in the possibility and *effectiveness* of acting on a world that was all lightness and malleability, a world that was just waiting for a strong will to take possession of it and change it utterly. Having been privy from their earliest conscious years to this historical upheaval, to this instant victory of action over the weight of the world, could only persuade the children of the lyric generation that they, too, had the power — even the mission — to translate their desires into action so that reality would give way whether it wanted to or not. They were like infants discovering new capabilities and never ceasing to marvel at them. To act — to make their mark on the world — became more than a task or duty; it was a kind of pleasure, a way of experiencing in concrete terms both the lightness of the world and the extent of their own power.

This joy was all the more intense because that action always went hand in hand with an unassailably clear conscience. Knowing they were the harbingers of the future and convinced they embodied what was best and most precious in the world, these young people did not doubt for a moment the value and legitimacy of their contributions or their projects. It was clear to them, as it was indeed to most of their elders, that if they acted, not only would they succeed in their aims, but the consequences would necessarily be for the best. Action, in other words, provided its own moral justification. It was, by definition, good and innocent, sincere and just, because it expressed the desires and the vitality of these princes of the world creating in their own image, out of the purity of their hearts, the kingdom they were promised from the moment of their birth.

Their convictions — the feeling that they occupied the centre of society and constituted an elite embodying the needs and aspirations of all, that there was joy and ease in action, and that they possessed power and legitimacy — were linked to the circumstances of their arrival in the world and would deeply mark the mentality of the lyric generation and inspire it for decades to come. To belong to this generation would always, one way or another, mean to see oneself and be seen as one who holds power in the world and virtually unlimited mastery of the circumstances of one's own life and that of the community as a whole. It would mean, to cite Kundera, to feel the steering wheel of history vibrating in one's hands and having only to grasp it in order to dictate the road to follow.

This feeling of mastery was another trait that distinguished the children of the lyric generation from those who came later — that is, both the last cohort of the baby boom, who would not turn twenty until the end of the seventies, and the youth of the eighties and nineties, made up in large part of their own children. For these new generations of young people, in fact, the world would seem once again like the wall I described earlier: a closed, often hostile place that would escape their grasp, and to which they would have to adapt as best they could in order to make a place for themselves within it. When they arrived there, they would not have the privilege of feeling they were already its masters. On the contrary. The world had already been shaped and ordered according to the wishes of the older baby boomers, and they were still at the controls and firmly in command. The world would have become unalterable.

And so the youth that came after the lyric generation had no other choice but to sit at the back of the bus and quietly allow themselves to be driven along the road of history, hoping there would be no accident, for if there were it knew it would be the first and doubtless only victim. To a large extent, these young people would find themselves in an even more hopeless position than their grandparents and the young of all periods preceding the reign of the lyric generation, whose destiny would prove, once again, to be unique, with no parallel in the past, and no counterpart, it would appear, in the foreseeable future.

LYRIC UNREST

Nothing can prevail against the power
of negation, scorn and primal prideful energy
that stirs in the heart of someone young
and ambitious who as yet has done nothing in life.
What strength there is in having done nothing!

Paul Valéry
My Faust

Although we would have to wait for the second half of
the seventies and the beginning of the eighties to see the lyric
generation take effective control of society, by looking at the
previous decade, we could already get a foretaste of what was
to come, a sort of dress rehearsal, the first public appearance
of the future masters of the world: the student movement.

For a long time, of course, students in the Western world
had constituted a particularly noisy and visible pressure
group, one that had no true power of its own, but was able
to act on established authority with a force that had to be
reckoned with, if only because these same individuals would
soon become citizens in their own right and join the ranks of

the ruling elite. In the meantime, their role was that of a prod, a stimulus: to make the voice of the future and new generations heard, to push for action and radical measures, and to do so all the more blithely, all the more strenuously, if the likelihood of their demands being realized in the short term was just about nil. And so their platforms and demonstrations were a cross between social gatherings and ritual magic.

The student movement of the sixties, as manifested in most European countries and especially in the United States, culminating with May 1968 in France, presented many of the same features. It was still, in large part, adolescent in nature, and it expressed the impatience and spirit of rebellion characteristic of that age. The students of the period repeated the actions of their predecessors: they stamped their feet, they raised their voices, and they made spectacles of themselves by venting their excess libido in public.

However, it would be a disservice to the deeper meaning of this phenomenon not to see how different it was from student movements of the past — and from those of today, if such things still exist.

The first difference, as always, was quantitative. Where numbers were concerned, the student population of the sixties had nothing in common with that, say, of the thirties or fifties. Not only did the baby boom considerably increase the number of young people, and the proportion of the population they represented, but the percentage of students within this group was much greater than in the past, even in countries that had not been affected by the baby boom. At one time a privilege accorded a small band of fortunate individuals, student status for the youth of this period was so widespread and accessible that it came to be regarded as the normal avenue for entry into society.

There were many reasons for this change: the economic climate and the ideology of the welfare state, certainly, but also the parental concern to ensure the success and self-fulfilment of their children and to provide for them what they themselves had never had. To that we may add the lengthening period of schooling and the wider access to higher levels of education, all of which helped to swell the student contingent, raise their average age, and render the student experience less transitory and ephemeral than in the past.

The students at the heart of the lyric generation were indeed still a minority. But it was a minority that saw itself quite differently from those of the past, and that related to its nonstudent contemporaries in a new way.

The students of earlier days retained, for the most part, the characteristics, attitudes, and interests of the privileged class from which they stemmed and to which they continued to belong; their student status was one of the signs of this privilege. Unlike other young people their age, who were workers or apprentices, students had the air of the well-to-do and behaved as such. Studies pursued beyond the secondary, or even elementary, level were not only a luxury, they were a sign of affluence, a proof of eminence, of not being part of the majority, the majority of youth in particular.

This becomes obvious when one examines, for instance, the student movements of the thirties, for whom the surrounding social, political, and ideological uneasiness offered excellent opportunities. Aside from the energy and vitality that animated them, what characterized most of these movements, certainly in French Canada, was their reactionary nature, the passion with which they demanded not revolution or the disruption of society, but rather a return of order, discipline, and the "fundamental values" dear to conservative tradition. These aspirations took the forms of an obsessive yearning for a leader, the condemnation of democratic institutions considered a source of anarchy and spawning grounds for mediocrity, and the glorification of the elites, who would keep in check the savagery emerging from the rising masses, who were uneducated and devoid of moral sense. The committed students of the time were those who waged battle most vehemently with the communist devil and the domination of "international Jewry," who denounced most ardently the relaxation of moral standards or the influence of subversive books and films, who worked tirelessly for the reestablishment of a society that would be "healthy" and properly hierarchical, who, in short, most courageously defended the power and privileges of the class to which their fathers belonged — even against other factions of youth.

This student agenda survived, more or less, until the beginning of the sixties. Philosophies changed, of course, but the relationship between students and other youth did not. Always students saw themselves less as representatives of the young than as their mentors, less as the cutting edge of youth within society than as those who would bring the cutting edge of society to the young. The student movement, in short, saw itself as what it in fact was: a pool of future politicians, prominent citizens, prelates, and business leaders, a nursery for the elites of tomorrow.

There were traces of this past in the student movement of the sixties, but they were less visible, camouflaged or eclipsed by an entirely new student consciousness, which emerged in part because the students' position vis à vis other young people had radically changed. Because of their numbers, and because they now represented more varied backgrounds thanks to the democratization of education, the students were no longer, or at least no longer appeared to be — no longer felt themselves to be — creatures of privilege. They were now seen and saw themselves not only as young people exclusively, but as that segment that embodied and experienced most exactly and most completely the problems, frustrations, and hopes of their generation. The distinction between being young and being a student disappeared, and they became virtually one and the same: youth was the student world.

Objectively, such an equivalence is, of course, false. But where the new student ideology of the time was concerned, its truth was beyond question. It was in the name of all youth that the student leaders and student unions proclaimed their grievances and demands. Youth for them was no longer just a sector of society that had to be made to conform to a certain program or social doctrine. Youth was now their base and support; no longer the object of their initiatives, but the wellspring from which they would flow and the reservoir where they would constantly gather strength and be renewed.

The conviction that they represented an entire generation, that they were invested with all the power and spirit of postwar youth, was widely shared by the student activists of those years, and it goes far to explain the peremptory, strident tone of their speeches and actions.

Among the important objectives that student leaders and ideologues proposed to their followers, the first concerned the student condition itself: it had to be improved and "liberated," which was the hope, in particular, of so-called student militants. They wanted to take control of their own education, which meant no more submission to the authority of teachers, or to society as a system that regulated and controlled their apprenticeship. Education, from this perspective, would no longer be something imposed from the outside, but instead would be an autonomous process, an experience directed by individual students in response to their own needs, which they would themselves define.

In the same way, the goals of education would no longer be to prepare students for life, responsibility, or a future career; nor would they be to correspond to the requirements of the economy or to norms established by tradition. Programs would have to be organized in terms of the present good of the students and their freely chosen expectations and options. Students were no longer the passive recipients of values and knowledge instilled from the outside, like prisoners being rehabilitated. Rather their role was to refuse indoctrination and to take themselves in hand. They were the primary managers of their own development, since they were the only ones who truly knew themselves. It was up to them to decide what was good for them and to pass judgement on their successes and failures.

In Quebec, and doubtless elsewhere, as well, a consequence of this non-functional view of education was the leap in popularity, in colleges and universities, of subjects that up to that point had been considered the least useful and the least realistic, such as the social sciences (sociology, political science, anthropology, psychology) and, not far behind, literature and the arts. Higher education, whose goal in the past had been to develop professionals and to pass on a body of knowledge, now became a hub of criticism and reflection that was removed from society rather than subservient to its needs, concerned with the assessment and reform of the real world rather than its consolidation. The typical students of the thirties or forties, doing dissections or consulting the civil code, were replaced by discoverers of Marx (or rather, Marcuse) and Freud (or rather, Reich and Carl Rogers) who harboured grand designs for society. Students discussed these at considerable length in the evenings with their friends, and the next day penned fiery articles for the student paper.

Within the universities and colleges thus divested of their former utilitarian vocation, the student universe appeared increasingly autonomous and self-sufficient, a world apart with no essential connection to any other entity, able to manage its own affairs and to establish its own norms and priorities. The student condition, seen until then as nothing more than an extension of childhood or a kind of antechamber for adult life, now was perceived — and experienced — as a state of being or station in life equivalent to youth itself. And so the student world came to consider itself, and to be considered, one of the sectors of public life, with interests and rights equal to those of the working class or the business world.

These demands for autonomy went hand in hand with another argument typical of student ideology at that time, one that at first glance might appear contradictory, but was not at all. It is what I would call, for lack of a better word, the demand for *protection,* which required that society, whose guardianship students claimed to reject, make available to students everything they needed to live and fulfil their role. In concrete terms, it meant free education, an increase in resources and budgetary allocations for education, and even "student pay" or a "study allowance," which was one of the movement's primary objectives at the time. Of course, to justify these demands, students drew liberally on democratic and egalitarian rhetoric. But what really inspired them was the model of the privileged classes: although they were making no contribution for the moment to the production of wealth for society, the students still felt it was their right to absorb a large part of it and demand that their livelihood, even their well-being, become a public priority. In other words, they demanded what young people before them had regarded as a burden to be thrown off as soon as possible: material dependence on their parents.

If we wanted to sum up student consciousness of the sixties, which was a microcosm for the youth mentality of the time, especially for that group of "advanced" young people who made up the lyric generation, we would have to resort again to the self-image I have been trying to define since the beginning: innocent, sovereign, ubiquitous; imbued, consciously or not, with a conviction so deeply rooted it had almost become instinctive that they not only constituted a separate world, a society within society, but a world that was purer and more genuine, a better society, and one that as a result had the right (or the duty) not to assimilate but to reap benefits on all sides. They had to be and to remain, in short, the children of light, charged with the world's salvation. There was nothing more natural, in these circumstances, than to want to negotiate a contract with parents and educators that would do away with their authority, yet require them to spend continually more.

This sort of messianism is nowhere more evident than in the other great project of the student movement of the time: to remake the world. Student militants were not content to act in their own domain — that of education and the student condition. They very quickly opened a second front that soon became their principal field of battle: society itself — its institutions, the way it functioned and shared out power and wealth, the defining of its goals. And so, they developed an ideology and student activism that was universal in its application, and whose aim was the transformation and *overall* restructuring of society.

This ideology and activism found support in a student population that was more visible, more certain of its strength, and more effective than ever, and deeply marked the history of those years. There were epic battles between students and the police on American campuses and during the Democratic Convention in Chicago, a student uprising at the Mexican Olympics, and of course, the events of May 1968 in France. In Quebec, this mobilization took on a nationalist cast; but over and above their demonstrations for a "McGill français" or against State bilingualism (Bill 63), what the students were after was a sweeping change in the conduct and organization of their society.

Whatever the country and whatever the sociopolitical context in which they took place, these rebellions have been the object of a great many accounts and analyses, of which one of the most complete is still *Génération* by Hervé Hamon and Patrick Rotman. Certain aspects of the phenomenon provide valuable insights into the distinctive psychology of the lyric generation, spearhead of the whole movement.

In the first place, we are struck by how thoroughly optimistic the attitudes and outlook behind this militancy were. Not for an instant did the young rebels fear for their cause or doubt that they were in the right and that the consequences of their actions would be beneficent. While other social movements — revolutions, workers' uprisings, peasant revolts — may have been driven by rage or despair, this one was all jubilation, full of laughter, sexual freedom, and a euphoria that made it seem less a struggle or an insurrection than an enormous carnival.

There were at least two reasons for this optimism. First, in turning the world upside down without violence or bloodshed, youth experienced firsthand the reality and scope of its

own power. Armed with the knowledge that they were beautiful and free and had good fortune on their side, these young
gods and goddesses seized history's steering wheel with both
hands and plunged into the world, prepared to destroy everything in their path. "The new innocence," proclaimed *A
Treatise on How to Live for the Use of Young Generations,* "is
the lucid construction of an annihilation." And second, they
put to the test the lightness and inconsistency of the world
before them, which they could topple, dismiss, or ignore at
their will, for it had neither the means nor the right to truly
defend itself.

This is the source of another important feature of student
militancy in the sixties: the extremism, or rather "maximal-
ism," typical both of its doctrine and the demands it made on
what I have called the second front — the world. The
students' confidence in their own strength and their faith in
the future constantly spurred them on to greater feats of
daring, encouraged them to make more and more radical
demands, and broaden indefinitely the horizons of their
action. Very soon, it was not a specific change or the correc-
tion of some injustice or the rejection of a taboo that they
desired. It was the dissolution of everything, a new beginning.
Not the overturning of some regime, but the elimination of
the very idea of power. Not the recognition of workers' rights,
but the end of work. Not reform, but *revolution.*

The lyric generation derived from all that a concept of
political and social action that it would take a long time to
unlearn, if ever. In its view, only total renewal, the will to
destroy and start all over again, constituted a project that was
legitimate and worthy of marshalling its energies. Fascinated
by radicalism, it had and would continue to have the greatest
of difficulties entertaining the sort of moderate and imperfect
measures common in political life. All that was not rupture

and a new beginning was viewed as obstructionism; whatever was not revolutionary was reactionary.

The word "revolution," in the student consciousness of the time, had almost religious significance. It referred not so much to a more or less distant *objective,* to an event that would take place in the future and put an end to history or totally change its course, as to an ongoing open-ended and permanent *process,* a new way to make history and experience it in the present tense, to be and act in the world through constant agitation and a rejection of all forms of stability in favour of a perpetual state of flux. Understood in this way, the "revolution without a name," as Vaneigem called it, had no conclusion or foreseeable result; it began again every God-given day, for the slightest hiatus would be a betrayal, would transform it into its opposite: order, heaviness, and to all intents and purposes, death.

This mystic vision of revolution, which was like the aggravated impatience and rebelliousness typical of adolescence translated into a collective furore, was largely responsible for the difficult relations between the student movement and other revolutionary organizations at the time. On the one hand, student activists felt a certain solidarity with the traditional left, to the extent that they were a destabilizing factor in society. But on the other hand, any party or well-defined program was suspect, as were the discipline it imposed in the present and the new order it would establish in the future, an order that might turn authoritarian and therefore be dangerous. For radical youth, to see revolution as did the old left — as an instrument, as simply a means of taking power — was to betray the true revolution and to divert it from its purpose, the perpetuation and radicalization of its own movement.

Such a difference in orientation could only allow for relatively ambiguous and tentative tactical alliances between students and "certified" revolutionaries or, in the case of Quebec, between students and those I have called the frustrated reformers. These groups, in fact, were never able to count on student militancy, which was pure militancy — free and spontaneous action — and therefore, by definition, unpredictable and impossible to control. They would make use of it, of course, and take advantage of it, but they could never make it part of their plans; it would never serve their purposes. The students and young people would always elude them or outflank them one way or another, when they did not outright oppose their initiatives in the name of what was considered a higher or more authentic concept of the Revolution.

Cooperation would seem to have been easier between the student movement and the new left, that is, the various currents of emancipatory thought and action that were associated less with the traditional working class than with the new "minority" voices that were then being mobilized. These included peoples oppressed by the West — blacks, the Vietcong, Cubans — and within the Western world itself — societal outcasts such as welfare recipients, the chronically unemployed, immigrants, prisoners, psychiatric patients, and other victims of the system. (Women's liberation was not yet on the agenda, nor were gay rights.) In Quebec, the nationalism of the sixties benefited greatly from this tendency of students to identify with all who, held back by the established order and therefore potentially revolutionary, had as yet no specific philosophy and were given instead to spontaneous outbursts that were unrelated to any preconceived programs or strategies.

Here again, however, the alliance was not without ambiguity. It is clear that student participation played an important role in raising the profile of these emancipatory movements and in the real gains they were able to make. It is also certain that the youth movements helped in the "consciousness raising" and the limited, but undeniable liberalization of society at that time. But we may also ask to what degree the failures and rapid collapse of these same movements was attributable in large part to their being submerged in and taken over by student ideology and activism.

For student militancy, when it launched its assault on the second front and set out to change the world, could in no way present a definite program or series of goals. Rather, its program, if we were to try to define it, was strictly speaking not social, political, or economic; it was "metaphysical" or "cosmological," that is, so vast, so absolute, that it became impossible to express, except through slogans or scraps of discourse that were poetic or magical, and whose media of preference were banners and graffiti. It was, as a song of the period put it, a "rebellion without a cause," resistance without a focus, unwilling and doubtless unable to target any positive objective, any concrete utopia towards which and in the name of which it expended its efforts.

This is perfectly clear from the account by Hamon and Rotman of the events leading up to May 1968 in France. In the beginning, the movement's political orientation was quite coherent. It was Marxist-Leninist in inspiration, and it held to this orientation, for a time, in its public declarations and some of its demonstrations. But as the decade went on, this program lost its relevance. Militants of the "proletarian revolution" gave way to Trotskyites and Maoists, then to *enragés* and "situationists," and finally to pure amateurs of tumult, who wished only to indulge their taste for fun and furore, and their need for strong sensation. "Power, power struggles, tactics," write the authors of *Génération*, "they couldn't care less. The true revolution is to have a ball without waiting for the revolution."

At the time, these revolutionary practices were often referred to as "contestation," a word that acquired a new, intransitive meaning, signifying an attitude rather than an action.

Contestation was the revolution in action, the day-to-day ground attacks against quarry that were always changing, always new. It was lyric guerrilla warfare; so as not to "be had," that is, to feed their impatience, keep alive the sense of their own power, and ensure that the party would never end, the militants sought out pockets of resistance wherever they could, flushed out whatever was weighty or stable, and fired on whatever moved, or rather, on what did not move at all. Professors, parents, bosses, political leaders, intellectuals, institutions, traditions — everything and everyone that represented order or stability — were viewed as oppressors and usurpers, and as boring to boot. As such, they deserved to be criticized, if not brought down. Not necessarily so that something better might be put in their place, but simply to clean house, that the world might change, that everything might become lighter, that this mad dialectic — this intoxicating beat that was to be the rhythm of history — might never come to a stop.

The enemy, under these circumstances, were the old. And the old were automatically and necessarily ensconced, entrenched, unredeemable, and fascist. They were fossils who defended the old world and lived off the fat of the land, or, if they seemed to capitulate, did so only as a ruse, the better to co-opt what was a threat to them. They were always singled out in the protests, one of whose features, too often forgotten, was the instinctive, almost visceral rejection of the older generation: *"Don't trust anyone over thirty!"*

Such attitudes — reducing people to what defines them

biologically (age), glorifying what is intact and pure (youth), showing signs of rote suspicion and contempt, refusing to listen or to discuss, as well as showing intolerance, impertinence, and aggression — came very close, at times, to a kind of racism. But what I think defines the militants better is what could be called their *aristocratic* mentality, that is, their conviction that they belonged to a distinctive, nobler, more perfect caste and that their superiority gave them the right to be arrogant and to treat the old, the "lower caste," as undesirable or inferior. The members of an aristocracy, wrote Tocqueville, knew that "they in no way resembled all the others; they did not think or feel in the same way, and they could barely believe they were part of the same humanity. In no way, then, could they understand what the others experienced, or judge them for what they were." The militants could only judge the old in terms of their own standards and the superiority that they knew was theirs.

One could say that this rejection of the old, this war on the pigs, was only a response to another form of rejection, another kind of discrimination, or racism, this one institutionalized and secular: the exclusion of the young, the silence imposed on them down through the ages, and their domination by the old in the organization and life of the community. This argument is typical of lyric sophism. Its intent is to interpret student militancy, as well as every youth phenomenon of the sixties, as a power struggle, as a kind of civil war pitting one adversary against another, each determined to win control of society, and it obscures everything that was distinctive about these times. Granted, the outbreak of militancy occurred when, in almost every country, the euphoric climate of the beginning of the sixties was giving way to a certain gloom and stiffening of the established order. In the United

States, it was the age of Nixon, with the assassination of
Martin Luther King and the bogging down of the Vietnam
war; in France, the Gaullist regime seemed impossible to
dislodge and was mired in routine; in Czechoslovakia, Rus-
sian tanks entered Prague; while in Quebec, the Quiet Revolution had run out of steam and was now called Jean-Jacques
Bertrand. The horizon, in short, compared to what it had
been under Kennedy, under de Gaulle at the beginning, or
under Lesage seemed indeed to be closing in, and stasis and
heaviness were gaining ground.

But to say that society was rejecting youth, that it was
inclined to exclude it or box it in, thus obliging the young to
take by force the territory that had been refused them, was a
leap that only the maximalist rhetoric of the time could make.
In fact, despite the increased rigidity, never had young people
had so much leeway, so much room to manoeuvre, so many
resources on which they could draw. For the most part, the
reforms they asked for were obtained without delay, in education especially. They were given the right to vote even before
they demanded it. They had fewer obligations, and many
minor freedoms long requested and denied: the freedom to
have clothes, reading matter, music, a career, and a sex life of
their choosing; the freedom not to go to church; and even the
freedom to break definitively with their family and community. In other words, never had a generation of young people
been blessed with such latitude and such ease; never had a
generation been so little oppressed, so rarely denied, by its
elders.

According to the student ideology of the time, and to the
tender memories we still foster of the sixties, if the young of
that period were obliged to resort to militancy and protest, it
was because they wanted their place in the sun in order to
make the world more open and humane. But it would be

more accurate to say it was because the young already occupied so generously their place in this world that they were able to discover the giddy pleasures of militancy and protest, through which they expressed less their revolt than their confidence and joy. Their insubordination, then, was not a demand for freedom, but a sign of this freedom itself.

NARCISSUS MULTITUDINUS

In my account of the student movement and the turmoil associated with the sixties, there was one element lacking, without which it is impossible to understand the climate of this period or to reconstitute the mentality of that generation. I call this element demographic narcissism.

The term *narcissism,* made popular by Christopher Lasch in particular, has been used liberally to describe the condition of the modern individual: turned in upon himself, preoccupied with his image and his personal growth, subservient to an inflated, exalted ego, and therefore prey to unremitting solitude and instability. It seems to me that narcissism was another of the lyric generation's typical traits, linked like the others to the circumstances surrounding this generation's entry into the world and like them making its spectacular, even groundbreaking debut in the sixties, which further enhanced that period's archetypal character.

We generally think of Narcissus as sitting alone at the edge of a pool, gazing at his own reflection, hearing only the echo of his own voice, and neither wanting or knowing how to love anyone but himself; the world around him is a desert, and there is no other living soul in sight. In this sense, we might say that the narcissistic attitude is the exact opposite of what the lyric generation experienced; so large were its numbers that any retreat into the self, any individual solitude, would have been impossible.

That is why I prefer to speak of demographic, or collective, narcissism. The retreat into the self — contemplating and enjoying their own image — was a trait not of the individual but of the group, not of each person in particular but of the homogeneous, teeming whole, which felt both distinct from all others and alone in the world. This was already implicit in the feeling of centrality I spoke of earlier; given their mass, which made other groups seem insignificant, and given the adoring attention bestowed on them by these same groups, who were unwilling or incapable of offering them any resistance, this generation not only felt it was different and impossible to assimilate, but had the impression that only it was truly there, only it was truly *real* in the social world that it inhabited. It filled that world to the point where the world seemed to reflect it completely.

For these young people, collective narcissism was a concrete given. Because of their numbers, they lived their lives as and among a crowd. Whatever they did, whatever they experienced, whatever they thought, invariably there was a throng of them doing, experiencing, and thinking it. Their environment, their natural surroundings, was the crowd. Each of their experiences, each of their so-called individual choices, assumed the form and dimensions of a wave, and was fragmented into an infinite number of similar experiences and choices made *at the same moment* by other young people their age, under identical conditions and for the same reasons. Their way of dressing, taste in music and reading, and optimism or rebellion were shared by thousands, millions, of other young people who, like them, made up that most dense and visible group; other groups were virtually weightless, seemed not to exist, or at least were unable to compete or to offer any opposition.

But narcissism, for individuals immersed in this multitude, also meant never encountering anyone other than people similar to themselves, people who were the same age, wore the same clothes, listened to the same records, went to the same clubs, and shared the same view of the world, the same concerns, the same expectations. The "other" was no longer a different, foreign other, someone to face down and in whose presence I had to consent to sacrifice part of what I was. There was no longer any other, only an enormous *we*, identical to myself, that welcomed me, enfolded me, was an extension of myself, and authenticated and magnified every moment of my life. To be at once reassured and exalted, I needed only to look around me and feel the hearts of my peers beating as one to the rhythm of my own, and I needed to have only one desire, one wish: to remain forever among them, with them, in their midst, in the same procession, in the same drift of history. To live was to live in a crowd, be multitudinous, face-to-face with oneself in the midst of all.

From its initiation into public life, this generation thus acquired the habit of melting into an enormous assembly that was both the individual's own projection and his obliteration, his reflection and his oppressor. Any experience not lived in a crowd or not involving the complicity of millions of others seemed devoid of reality and of value. Any desire, any opinion, any feeling, had meaning only if it was shared with an infinite number of other, identical young people, all of whom identified with it uniformly and in a united fashion, to distinguish themselves from their elders.

This awareness of number, this feeling of being carried along by something greater and more powerful than themselves, this statistical sense of their own identity, would be another important component of the personality and spirit of the lyric generation (and of the baby boom). No other generation before or after would have the same sense of its own cohesion and demographic weight; none would see itself to the same degree as a compact and united host, linked by an absolute harmony of experiences and points of view. This feeling of belonging was so deeply ingrained in the lives of these young people that it came to supplant any other characteristic they might have used to define themselves. So it was for socioeconomic differences — which lost much of their importance and no longer prevented young people, whether they were the children of working- or middle-class parents, from the city or the country, from having the same tastes, the same desires, the same language, the same relaxed and gracious demeanour. The same went for differences of language or culture, which also tended to disappear or fade into the background in the face of this rising tide that sociologists referred to as the new youth "subculture." This subculture was the same from one end of the West to the other, with identical references and, beyond a few fairly superficial local divergences, had the same values and the same models.

An age class presenting the appearance of a classless society, a new International based on the rejection of linguistic and cultural barriers, the lyric generation, with its cult status and moral imperative of similitude, would thus be the first totally democratic generation in history. It was not just a matter of sharing, but of the disappearance of the individual into the whole, the absorption of the separate, autonomous person, once posted proudly at the centre of his consciousness as on an island whose shores he jealously guarded, into a vague, limitless entity that was this group to which he now belonged.

In the sixties, this meant being young and beautiful,

brimming over with energy, and having the world to oneself as much as one desired it. The narcissism of this period was essentially joyous and confident. It was crowds of young people dancing in celebration of their own beauty and power, heralding their arrival in the world, and seeing themselves reflected in the eyes, voices, and body language of one another. This dimension, it seems to me, is what gave student militancy its unique carnival atmosphere, like a vast, roaring party on the scale of an entire society. With their sit-ins, their marches, and the great "motiveless festival" of May 1968, as Hamon and Rotman called it, what kept the young militants going and made them ever more sure of themselves was not simply the pleasures of subversion and their feeling of power. It was also, perhaps even more profoundly, the growing awareness of their generational solidarity: their sense of wonder in experiencing together the same emotions, of confronting together the same "oldsters," of encountering together the same frustrations and the same desires. Theirs was the joy, in short, of seeing themselves in each other and of being in love with what they saw. They talked to each other, touched, held hands, walked in step, responded as one: they were among their own, they were legion, and they were at last alone.

In their militancy, the joy of belonging went hand in hand with rebellion against the other side, whose presence reinforced and enhanced this joy, for it required the young to form a solid front, to stick even more closely together, in order to bolster the feeling of solidarity and mutual recognition. But theirs was a joy tinged with anger and negativity. To see *narcissus multitudinus* in its pure state, we must consider another aspect of the times that was just as typical and of which student militancy was perhaps only one offshoot — it was a bit more violent, a bit more conspicuous, but its motivation, when all is said and done, was the same.

I am referring here to what we might call the youth festivals, whose archetype remains the monster gathering of Woodstock, at Bethel in the state of New York, from the 16th to the 18th of August 1969. But Woodstock was only the most renowned of a long series of love-ins and similar events that took place in various countries between 1967 and 1972. In Quebec, aside from a few festivals modelled on those in the United States and England, it was the world fair in Montreal during the summer of 1967 that saw the explosion of youthful euphoria. Unique as they were, these events only concentrated into a few particularly intense moments what seemed to be the prevailing current of the entire decade, a current that was animated, agitated, and traversed from end to end by an immense upsurge of joy created by the advance of the new generation. This explains the powerful symbolic charge of these landmark events that punctuated an idyllic period when the lyric generation was most brilliantly itself.

These gatherings of young people were, like all festivals, gatherings *without a purpose,* that is, events that had no particular cause and no ideology, that protested against nothing, demanded nothing, and encountered no opposition. Pure events, in a way, they had no reason for being other than to occur in a certain place at a certain time in as spectacular a fashion as possible, and were well described by the new word coined with them in mind: "happenings."

The young gathered for the simple pleasure of gathering, of forming a crowd, of experiencing for a blessed moment — which might last several days — their affiliation with something larger and more fundamental than themselves. It was a kind of pilgrimage, and indeed, it was as wanderers that they came from all directions, backpacks on their shoulders and faith in their hearts, to converge on the little village of Bethel or the utopian islands of Man and His World, these young people all imbued with the same fervour and all certain that revelation was at hand.

But this revelation, the god they came to worship, had no icon and no sanctuary to represent it. For they carried within themselves what was best and most precious: their own youth. They had stripped themselves of everything, had left behind their parents, teachers, employers, and had travelled thousands of kilometres to bathe in these miraculous waters and to witness the spectacle of their teeming and triumphant generation. They had come to see and adore themselves.

That is why the most striking aspect of these festivals was always the enormous size of the crowds that attended them. This aspect alone, in fact, made the festival. The greater the number of pilgrims, the more impossible it became even to count them, and so the greater the faith, and the greater the exaltation. And the more heightened, too, was the feeling of belonging and fellowship, a feeling that fully accomplished that dissolution of the self, that plunge into *continuity* that Georges Bataille defined as the most sublime erotic experience. Submerged in a crowd that continued to grow and spread out on all sides, each participant felt his identity blur bit by bit, open up, break free from its confines and disperse, until it was soon only an echo of this enormous pulsing body that was at once his own and that of all.

That is also why these festivals were not just accompanied, but impregnated, ordered, and ritualized by two elements that determined the liturgy: rock music and drugs. Rock was the sacred music for the cult devoted to the multifold Narcissus, the perfect incarnation of its spirit and of the miracle they were seeking. It was a music of trance. But more specifically, it was a music of *collective* trance, not there to be listened to, but to ordain a kind of possession, which required the annihilation of the individual and his absolute, immediate

surrender to the rule of a rhythm and sound that occupied all
of space, both within and without. Rock was never as pure or
as powerful as when it resounded through a crowd, engulfing
it, transporting it, fusing it with its own clamour, and becoming its pulse, its soul laid bare and scattered to the winds.
In that respect rock was not unlike military music, differ-
ing from it, however, in that, far from disciplining the movements of the crowd it controlled and working to enforce
conformity, rock magnified the disorder and diversity, and
created a pure mass, a swarming, unruly aggregate, all the more
forceful and tightly bound in that it permitted, required even,
tumult and confusion. Between a military march and a rock
tune, there is the same consistency and the same deviation —
the same progression, let us say — as between a principle of
Newtonian physics and a modern law of probability: both
create order and coherence, but one does it by eliminating
variants, the other by multiplying them ad infinitum.

Trance is also an effect of drugs: an individual trance,
certainly, with its loss of self and access to an artificial paradise,
but a collective trance as well. The use of marijuana and
hashish, or even harder drugs, ceased in the sixties to be a
solitary experience as had been the case in the past for poets
and artists such as Baudelaire or Henri Michaux, and became
a social activity, practised and celebrated in a crowd, a rite that
led people to "blow their minds," to break out of their
isolation and disappear body and soul into the throng. The
psychedelic "trip" was always a group tour.

Woodstock, Expo 67, and the other youth festivals were
exceptional moments, of course, as were all the great pilgrim-
ages and religious occasions. It was their very rarity, in large
part, that conferred on these occasions such renown and
transformed them into such intense and revelatory events.
But the cult continued beyond these privileged moments. It

survived all through the period, both in public and private life, sustained at first by the pervasiveness and omnipresence of rock, which functioned as a permanent sacrament and constant reminder of revealed truth. For even heard in private, within the four walls of a room, or later through the earphones of a Walkman, rock was always a music of the many and of joyous depersonalization. And the same could be said of drugs. Even when consumed alone or in secret, they retained all their eucharistic power, freeing the user from himself and providing him with the comfort of being linked with his community, the mystic body of young people his age.

But the perpetuation of the cult and its rituals also required a specialized caste, whose functions were properly sacerdotal: *hippies,* monks of the youth movement, whose role was always and everywhere, through their acts and their demeanour, to attest to the presence and power of god. The hippie attitude and moral stance, which emerged in California during the sixties and quickly spread throughout every country, was not unlike a form of priesthood. It involved renouncing any other quality, any other definition of the self, even one's name, in favour of the unique virtue of being young, in other words, beautiful and pure, innocent, free of the world, and a harbinger of its renewal.

Just as the priest is a believer more believing than others and entirely devoted to his faith, so the hippie was a young man or woman entirely dedicated to youth. And like the priest vis à vis ordinary believers, his vocation was not to set himself apart from other young people, but to resemble them as faithfully as possible, in heightened fashion, reflecting back to them a purified image of themselves, divested of everything that did not represent their deepest truth. Unlike the tramps and hobos of the past, hippies were not marginal, or if they were, their marginality was an extreme expression of what all the youth of the time wanted for themselves. Living in small nomadic groups as did the disciples of St. Francis of Assisi long ago, or in communes like those of Bernard of Clairvaux — one would be hard-pressed to find among them any hermits or cenobites — they talked to the flowers and birds and preached by example their peaceful crusade against the vices of the time. Hippies were, in fact, the heralds of the lyric generation, who recognized themselves in them, venerated them, imitated them, adopted their look, and dreamed of their freedom, just as did the faithful with regard to their priests and saints. For the hippie spirit, or message, was only the projection or systematization of the spirit and message embodied in the entire lyric generation: the infinite lightness of the world, the ease of acting and being, the conviction that they constituted a new, better, and purer humanity, the joy of finding themselves alone together, identical to one another, and yet separate from the rest.

When today we look at pictures of hippies or at photographs taken during the great festivals that brought together the youth of the period, we are surprised, for we had hardly thought of it at the time, by the strange *resemblance* they had to one another. They all wore the same T-shirts, the same faded blue jeans, the same bandannas around their heads, and had the same bare feet. And the difference between males and females was barely discernible: they had the same open faces, unkempt long hair, and slim, supple bodies; they might have been the original Hermaphroditus. But the resemblance did not end with the body: it extended to their gestures, their attitudes, their facial expressions, and doubtless their thoughts. They all had the same expression, part enchanted, part impertinent; the same smile; the same ecstasy repeated a hundred, a thousand times. This swarm of individuals, some dancing and singing, others tapping their feet and clapping their hands, still others sleeping on the ground or embracing in the midst of the crush, soon seemed like one enormous being, reproducing itself identically to the end of time, reflected vertiginously in itself for as far as the eye could see. Now one can see what caused this impression of vertigo: in all this crowd there was not one foreign element, not a single face of some maturity, not a single elderly person. There is nothing untoward in the photograph, nothing to destroy the symmetry: everyone was the same age, everyone was young, and that is why everyone was so happy and so beautiful.

ETERNAL YOUTH

Everything I have said in the last two or three chapters and presented as typical of the lyric generation — its feeling of the lightness of the world, faith in its own powers, a tendency to see itself reflected in a group, the narcissistic affirmation of its own individuality — has always been true of adolescents. It is a hallmark of youth, whatever the generation or period, to think of itself as the centre of the world and to rebel. In this sense, the lyric generation invented nothing.

Still, the youth of the lyric generation cannot be compared with that of the generations preceding it. It was a youth with no restrictions, an absolute youth that, even if it did show all the ardour, beauty, and energy associated with the young of all generations, suffered none of the torment or frustration that are usually the lot of humans of that age. This generation experienced again what it had experienced in infancy: its youth was a reinventing of youth, in other words a youth lived under totally new conditions, unique in history, and indebted again to the lucky star under which it had the good fortune to be born.

For youth, when we think about it, is not a particularly enviable state. Indeed, it was never considered or experienced as such, either in so-called traditional civilizations, or for that matter in modern society up till the beginning of the sixties. A hybrid age, halfway between childhood and adulthood, a contradictory age marked by awkwardness and uncertainty, it is the time of the great transition that completes the process of mental and physical maturation begun at birth. Now fully formed, individuals take possession of all their faculties; they no longer need care or protection, and they can procreate, work, and think. Biologically, nature has completed her task and the individuals now have all they need to survive, to age, and to make their way towards death. In this sense, adolescence, particularly in its final years, represents a kind of perfection: never are the bodies of men or women as beautiful or their brains as supple as during that period when they emerge, as it were, from their chrysalis. At that moment, youth has something about it that is indeed divine.

But in times past, this divinity was a divinity in chains. For to be young also meant, paradoxically, not being able to deploy those immense resources. The biological maturity of youth had to contend with its social immaturity and impotence. The community, that is, the elders, could not grant these not yet competent individuals the right or the power to govern it or to transform it and, considering them minors, it continued to protect them and keep them under surveillance.

This contrast between maturity and impotence, between childhood completed and adulthood still inaccessible, between having the capacity for autonomy and being faced with a dependence that seemed never to end, resulted in young men and women being anxious and tormented. On the one hand, they felt ready to act and live on their own; on the other, their elders prevented them from doing so and kept them in the background. This explains their crises of existential solitude and revolt, their insubordination, and their dreams, which were all the more excessive in that the dreamers did not have to deal directly with the world, controlled as they were and carefully kept at a distance by their elders.

This accounts as well for the shame associated with the experience of youth. Young people internalized their social inferiority, blamed themselves for it, and felt a kind of guilt, or at the very least dissatisfaction, making them impatient to have done with this empty phase in life, this waiting period they found so demoralizing, so indistinguishable from youth itself. And so they tried to camouflage their immaturity and wanted nothing more than to be admitted into the circle of elders. They imitated them, adopted their language and behaviour, and tried to mix with them. In brief, they tried to forget and make others forget their youthful condition, their infirmity, their curse.

There was only one way to leave behind this state and redeem this fault: it was to be reborn, or to be truly born, by attaining a new maturity, social and cultural this time, which imbued the individual with the traditions, the values, and the wisdom that constituted the good of the community. This knowledge alone, and the assumption of responsibility for this knowledge, could make young people adults and citizens in the fullest sense of the word, and could merit them their freedom, the confidence and acceptance of their elders. Until this initiation, young people remained youth, that is, inferior members of the group, members who had no power because they had no responsibility, and who were always dependent and submissive.

The young had only one goal: to escape their youth. That does not mean that the young had no value. On the contrary, youth was a critical period of preparation, of transition, of progressive integration into the community; the period during which, according to Hannah Arendt, the child, this foreigner, this "savage" newly set down in the world, this potentially threatening element, became conscious of his surroundings, became acculturated, as we would say today, and thus became capable of playing a responsible role in society. It was, in short, a period of *apprenticeship*.

This word *apprenticeship* has a precise anthropological meaning, designating the process by which the young and inexperienced, who have not yet adopted the habits and customs of their milieu, little by little acquire them through observing and assimilating the example or the teachings of those who preceded them in life — parents, teachers, and elders. And there are two sides to the coin. On the one, individuals gain. As they discover new knowledge, habits, ways of doing things, and values, young people — the apprentices, the students, the sons or daughters, in short, the *novices* — add something to themselves they did not before possess; they "grow." But on the other, this gain entails a loss that is no less real, to the extent that any apprenticeship also implies a renunciation. This knowledge and these values are acquired by the young from others; they are imposed from the outside; their acquisition and their mastery demand a certain docility, if not submissiveness: individuals must not only recognize the authority of their teachers and through them that of the community, but must agree to bend to this authority, to silence their own desires and ideas, and to sacrifice part of their own identity while allowing the "other" access to themselves that would leave them changed.

It is this negative, or debit, side of apprenticeship — as a form of repression or sublimation — that is the concern of that great literary tradition called the "novel of education" or

Bildungsroman, which is also known as the "novel of apprenticeship." Its basic structure, which is always the same, has
something archetypal about it in that it corresponds to a
deep-rooted pattern in human existence. The structure has
three stages: (1) full of energy and desire, a young man leaves
his family and sets out to conquer the world; (2) his adventure, as it unfolds and as the young man becomes older,
quickly changes from one of conquest to one of trial; little by
little (or all at once, it's of no importance) the hero loses his
innocence and encounters the resistance of the world; (3)
finally, faced with adversity, in other words, the failure to
realize his ambitions, either the hero refuses to give them up
and has no other choice but to retire forever from the world,
or he agrees to surrender and to live in the world as it is; either
he sloughs off his youth and goes home (see *A Sentimental
Education)* or he remains young and dies (see *The Sorrows of
Young Werther).*

What is important in this schema is that the hero is *never*
victorious. Or rather, his victory never resides in the realization of his desire or in his preserving his initial innocence. He
experiences a sort of "awakening" or "coming down to earth":
an acceptance of the world's solidity and superiority. The
novel of apprenticeship chronicles the ordeal of facing reality:
the young man dies so that the mature one may be born; pure
desire founders, or even better, is transformed into awareness,
into knowledge of the world and of oneself-in-the-world;
poetry meets reality, and the age of prose begins.

What is different about youth as experienced by the firstborn of the baby boom — and this just about sums up everything I have had to say so far — is that it was *not* the novel of
apprenticeship youth had always been. More precisely, the lyric
generation had all the advantages of an apprenticeship, and

abundantly so, through the education it received and the benevolent attention lavished on it by adults; but it was spared the torments and frustrations of apprenticeship, the necessity of tempering desires and beating a retreat before the hard reality of the world. Everything was given to these young people and nothing was demanded or imposed in return. To justify their admittance into the adult world, they did not have to recognize authority or adopt the traditions of their predecessors; they did not have to show proof of their wisdom, or just cause for the confidence to which they laid claim. They did not have to give up their youth.

The reasons are easy to understand. They underlie the entire destiny of this generation. First, their enormous numbers created an imbalance and weakened the influence of older groups, making any effective control of the newcomers difficult. Traditional structures designed to receive and assimilate them — human and physical, as well as cultural and ideological — were overwhelmed.

But not all the concerns were quantitative. Even more crucial, perhaps, was the attitude of the elders themselves: their humility before their offspring, their absolute faith in the future the young generation represented, persuaded them to relinquish their control and drop their demands, and thus to lighten the youth of these children of light. The purpose of an apprenticeship was to ensure the world's continuity from generation to generation. But when this continuity is no longer desired, when one no longer wants the world to be what it was, then how and in the name of what could one require the newcomers to submit to and learn from the world before being allowed access to it?

Never has society offered so little resistance to its youth. Almost no one contested the centrality that the lyric generation attributed to itself. On the contrary, it was granted willingly and without opposition, when not *placed in their hands* before it was even requested. Take, for example, sexual mores. It is often said that the sixties and seventies saw a great sexual revolution that swept away old strictures and lavished on everyone a freedom, a spontaneity, and a right to erotic fulfilment never before witnessed. This is undeniable. But of what did this revolution consist, exactly? Since time immemorial, adolescence and youth have been periods of discovery and sexual experimentation and particularly intense years of trepidation and ecstasy, yes, but also of impatience and rebellion against established taboos and morals. Adolescence was thus, in sexual terms, a period of revolt, daring, and latent libertinism, a time of real or imaginary transgression of rules imposed by the community. But revolt always ultimately failed, and the young, however wanton they may have been, eventually learned the codes of the adult community and modified their behaviour. Sexual freedom, in other words, was a limited and temporary freedom that would sooner or later have to be renounced, a fact that increased and heightened both pleasure and guilt. What was new for the youth of the lyric generation was that this freedom was no longer restricted in any way. Not only did nothing oppose the acting out of adolescent desire, but the acting out became the norm, the standard model for any "balanced" sex life. Men of fifty, mothers of families, and priests, mesmerized by the happiness of these young lovers, suddenly discovered that they were frustrated, repressed, and lacking in fulfilment, and they rushed to renew their affiliation with the libidinal ardour of their youth — so much so that the young did not have to give up their zeal for new experience and sexual freedom, but rather saw that zeal become the new morality, the new code of behaviour accepted by the entire community.

What happened with sexual morals was the same thing that happened with rock music. While twenty or thirty years earlier, jazz had been frankly suppressed and had had to lead a semiclandestine existence for some time, rock was immediately welcomed outside its target audience by all of society, not just with tolerance and indulgence, but with an enthusiasm approaching that of the young rockers themselves. Within a few years, the sound of electric guitars would become the music of choice for family evenings, popular gatherings, political conventions, and religious services.

The experiences of the youth of the lyric generation might bear a resemblance, then, to a novel of *non*-apprenticeship, or an *anti*-novel of apprenticeship. In this story the hero is triumphant. He sets out to conquer the world, and the world, instantly, falls into his hands. He charges head-on at reality, and reality obeys his will. Experience, in this upside-down world, is only the confirmation and heightening of innocence, and prose can do nothing against poetry, which is all-powerful. It is a *lyric* apprenticeship.

Clearly, the consequences of avoiding this apprenticeship (adroitly or dishonorably, depending on one's point of view) were great. Especially for the lyric generation itself, whose youth was pure enchantment, pure adventure free of tribulation, and without end. For apprenticeship, as I have said, was not simply the happy or unhappy fate of youth; it was also the means by which one shed this youth, like a first skin that was too tender. Now the lyric generation could hardly conceive of the transitory character of youth, and it seemed as though its own could go on forever. Having become conscious of themselves as young people, having defined in those terms what united them and set them apart, having met nothing along the way that obliged them to slough it off, these young people held to youth as though it were their very soul, their deepest and most precious self. And so for a long time they would find themselves unable to leave it behind — or to acknowledge that it had left them.

Their youth, in short, would become *eternal.*

Part Three

THE AGE OF REALITY

TAKING CONTROL

Because the sixties and early seventies coincided with the moment when the lyric generation first burst on the scene and made such an impression on public life, these years were indeed unique in many ways. But if we seek a complete understanding of that generation's spirit and the special nature of its destiny, it would be wrong to restrict ourselves to this period alone. In truth, those years were but a prelude. They prefigured what was to come, laid the groundwork for it, and determined its broad lines and parameters. But one would have to wait for the following decade to see how everything that was bubbling away during that time of youthful ferment would be translated into action, and what form it would take. We would have to wait, in other words, for that human wave — or rather the crest of that wave, the lyric generation — to at last attain adulthood, take control of society, and set out to shape it according to its own views.

Such control existed already, insofar as youth set the tone for the preceding period and exerted considerable influence over its elders. But this control was moral in nature and as such remained indirect, which of course was a limitation. Although the lyric generation already constituted the centre of gravity for society, effective mastery of society continued to be elusive. They were adolescents, students, young adults, but they were still a generation of *minors;* rebellious, confident, demanding, impatient to act, but still dependent and, as a result, remote from the levers of power.

All this would change towards the end of the seventies and into the eighties. Now in their thirties and soon their forties, the postwar children, having left their parents and teachers, set out in life and took the future of the community in hand. They had passed beyond the gates of childhood and youth and now poured into the world itself; they were mature and had reached the age of independence, discovery, and accomplishment. They had attained the age of reality.

Beginning in the middle of the seventies, then, there began a new phase in the marvellous saga of the firstborn of the baby boom, which would continue to the present day and has not yet approached its end. Now free to live and act as they wished, the lyric generation would from this point on show what they could do, what their lucky star and the experience of their youth had prepared them for. This period would prove even more revealing than the sixties, since the spirit of the lyric generation would now be embodied not only in feelings, desires, and festivals, but in acts, facts, decisions, and concrete measures.

Already, the very fact that this generation was now in its prime had a tremendous impact. The overpowering effect that had distinguished this generation of young people since birth was no less evident when they all moved into the various spheres of social interaction: work, consumption, politics, and culture. Again, nothing transpired in a fashion consistent with the gentle ways in which things had always occurred before, when new adults negotiated a place for themselves slowly and often with difficulty, obliged as they were to contend with their predecessors, and only obtained that share of power that was their right as a result of patience and perseverance. The lyric generation came of age in a great tide. Not only did the newcomers make their presence felt immediately and everywhere, but they quickly succeeded in displacing their elders and carving out a territory equal in scale to their ambitions.

Everything was in their favour. Besides their numbers, as always, there was their level of education, which far exceeded that of their elders, and destined them quite naturally for the best positions; it made them a privileged group from the start, a group for which the others willingly made way. Their instinctive solidarity, the generational consciousness forged in their youth, united them, reinforced the common experience and desire that made them one, constantly reminded them they had been singled out from others, and ensured their separateness would continue.

But mostly the newcomers' strength resided in themselves: in the eternal youth with which they had been endowed. It was their lovingly conserved youth that enabled them to make so many and such extreme demands, and to expect from life and the world much more than their parents at the same age dared to desire. For the first time, to become adult did not entail a relinquishment or a tempering of one's hopes and dreams, but seemed to set the stage for their total realization, without any delay or compromise.

Their eternal youth was also a source of inspiration, confirming the newcomers in their mission, giving them a sense of their own power, and convincing them that they would do infinitely better than all those who had come before. It was their youth that made them so resolute and resourceful. It required them to act, yes, but it also called for them not to back off before those who were already there, to mistrust them, in fact, and to take control of all possible power as soon as they could.

And their conquest was not long in coming. Within a few years, the new generation had asserted control. It did so first, of course, by monopolizing a large number of influential positions in different spheres of public life, whether it was the economy, education, political institutions, or the media. It was the reign of the young executive and youthful, "dynamic" entrepreneur, the "yuppie" and the "golden boy," the new prof bubbling over with ultramodern theories and ideas, and the union official with his brand-new poli-sci degree; these young upstarts had all the answers. They had their elders trembling in their shoes and were relegating them to the glum contemplation of their own "level of incompetence," which, according to the convenient Peter Principle, they had now attained. The hour of renewal had arrived.

Clearly, the new adults did not all find themselves in positions of power from one day to the next. Many of them, the majority perhaps, occupied and would continue to occupy for the rest of their lives lesser posts. A good proportion would even remain on the margins, forever dependent; in other words, social and economic differences endured. So did sexual inequality. While women of this generation had much greater access to public and professional life than their mothers had, they continued to lag behind their male contemporaries. And of course, not all the power dropped automatically into the laps of the lyric generation as soon as they were of age. Their elders inevitably held on to a large part of it.

That being said, even if all decisions, and the responsibility for carrying them out, were not actually in their hands, from an ideological and moral point of view, the lyric generation had control of society from this time on. It was now up to them, and more and more up to them alone, to define and embody the values and norms for everyone. As soon as they attained adulthood and became citizens in their own right, their view of the world, their expectations, and the dissent to which they gave expression when they were young and which no one had ever obliged them to forego became those of the entire community.

The first explanation for this may be traced to the older adults, who had very little choice in the face of the robustness, assurance, and competence of the newcomers but to give up without a struggle. Either they abandoned ship and faded into the background or, if they wanted to retain some semblance of power, welcomed the new recruits with open arms, celebrated their arrival, enthusiastically endorsed their goals, and identified increasingly with their approach; in other words, they became young at heart, modern, "with it," and joined the ranks of the victors. For the elders, this sort of cooperation and admiring consent had long been second nature.

But the emerging adults' success in spreading their gospel arose also from the abundant energy and confidence that their new position afforded them. The very fact that they had now assumed control of their own affairs could only reinforce the feeling of centrality they had acquired in their youth, could only exaggerate their tendency to see themselves as the stewards of values and interests to which the entire community had given its tacit consent — and to act accordingly. Thus, rather than inclining them to temper their demands and to transform their morality of conviction into one of responsibility, as Max Weber would say, their newly won power provided the lyric generation with yet another means, more effective than any at their disposal up till then, of persuading themselves and others that the common good was consistent with the accomplishment of their own goals and the satisfaction of their own desires. To work for their own happiness, from now on, was to work for the happiness of all. And vice versa.

The lyric generation's control over the world coincided with the moment when it shed all traces of the polemic character it had displayed during the sixties, and its program — or rather its sensibility, needs, and aims, for they had now achieved mastery of the world — came to reign supreme.

The most common and clearest example we can provide concerns the evolution of politics between the beginning of the seventies and about the middle of the eighties, when the new adults became a very important part of the electorate, not only in terms of their numbers, but also because of the positions they occupied in the most active and influential spheres of political life: the parties, unions, pressure groups, and media. What was striking in this development was the extremely close correspondence between political orientation, which in theory is linked to the *overall* expectations of society, and the preoccupations of the *particular* age group that made up the lyric generation.

In general, Quebec government intervention during these years was characterized both by continuity and rupture. There was continuity, in that the process that began with the Quiet Revolution, an increasingly widespread and aggressive interventionism, carried on and was even accelerated. Also, government continued to widen the scope of its activities and to expand significantly its personnel and resources. But at the same time there was rupture: the top priorities of the sixties, centred around the creation and promotion of apparatus that would enhance the development of society as a whole (infrastructure, natural resources, heavy industry, education), were replaced by a growing tendency to oversee individuals themselves, that is, to support and protect their private welfare.

The lyric generation was amply rewarded by continuity

and rupture alike. Because its members were just entering the work force, it had everything to gain from the rapid growth of the public and parapublic sectors, which offered young graduates an abundance of well-paid positions with a great deal of power and respectability. But it benefited as well from the government's new priorities, since these priorities, as though by chance, coincided exactly with the lyric generation's *current* needs. Just as the state, during the sixties, had committed itself wholeheartedly to financing and reforming the educational system, in other words, to what was then important to children born just after the war, so it now expanded its activities to include, more and more, those areas that concerned the adult sector of society.

The most obvious example was health care, a sector that had been relatively neglected up till then and that suddenly became for the government — as for individuals who were beginning to age and wanted to preserve the energy of their youth — the great and unique undertaking of those years, on the same scale at least, in terms of effort and public investment that went into it, as education in the previous decade. As well, many questions that had never caused either the government or its electors to lose any sleep, such as rent control, property ownership, day care, divorce, abortion, consumer protection, automobile insurance, the financial markets, and the culture and entertainment industries, suddenly became issues of the greatest urgency, requiring the active involvement of public authorities whose "duty" it was to intervene "for the good of society." Understood: For the good of the age group that constituted, if not the majority of the population, at least that segment of it that was most numerous, united, and aware of its strength and priorities.

But such immediate benefits only represented one of the advantages the lyric generation derived from its hold on the state. There were many others that were more subtle. Not content to impose on the community as a whole the satisfaction of its needs, its members succeeded in transferring to the state a large part of the *responsibilities* they ought now to have assumed, or in any case, that adults had always taken upon themselves in the past. So it was in the field of health. For the time being, it was not these new adults who required care, since they were only thirty or forty years old and had been well nourished and vaccinated since early childhood. But free medical care would still be to their advantage, absolving them of the need to pay out of their own pockets for the care of their parents and children, who could not do without it. One could say as much of the (partial) subsidization of day-care centres by the state: who would it benefit, first and foremost, if not young couples now "burdened" with children?

The most striking example, however, remains the policies concerning "golden-agers," a delicate euphemism for the elderly. Aside from meagre monthly pension cheques, the state had never paid much attention to the aged in the past, leaving it up to families and charitable institutions to look after them. Now, all of a sudden, during the seventies, old age became a major concern of both the government and the media, and the target of new programs: a substantial increase in pensions, indexation, the opening of homes financed by the state, free drugs, and so on.

Certainly, such a change in direction might be explained in part by an increase in the number of old people and by a growing awareness of the lamentable living conditions for most of them. But to see it as a pure function of public sympathy or, since these programs were supported by the young adults, as a sign of altruistic affection for their elders would be to misread this sudden compassion for the old; it is better seen as a response on their part, through the medium of *their* state, to *their* problems with the old.

First of all, was the immediate problem that the aging of their parents posed, for they would have had to care for them were it not more convenient to place them in the hands of the community. It was no longer up to sons and daughters to look after those who had brought them into the world, but rather up to society as a whole, its taxpayers, administrators, and state employees. And so the politics of aging coincided exactly with the interests of the younger generation.

But these policies would also prove their worth in the long term by enabling young adults to prepare for their own golden age, to organize in advance, as it were, so that when it was time for them to retire, they would be spared as much as possible the misery and decay that were the lot of old people now. That is why the most significant of the new measures supposedly designed with the aged in mind were not those that affected the old people themselves, because they were already too old to profit from them, but those that would apply to young adults. These included the upgrading of public and private retirement plans and the introduction of retirement savings programs — putting money aside for your old age while reducing your income tax, and so paying less for the old today. Also included was the elimination of a compulsory retirement age, which was not retroactive (so that the old remained unemployed) and which occurred at a time when the lyric generation was well established in the work force (so that the reduction in the number of job openings that this measure created did not affect them). Such policies, in short, were not so much designed to reassure the elderly of today as the elderly of the future, who were lightening their own old age while they were still young.

Despite appearances, it would be inexact to see in this

sort of moulding of the state any conspiracy on the part of the new adults. Inexact and unjust, for far from consciously seeking to profit at the expense of others, they acted as they did with total candour, persuaded that the reforms they proposed or put into effect would benefit the entire community. There was no Machiavellian or egotistical motive on their part. On the contrary, they were absolutely sincere and well meaning. If they drew on public funds to defend their own interests, it was because they were convinced that these interests would lead to greater freedom and happiness for humanity. They were not looking to profit for themselves; they were remaking the world.

It was this same innocence that a few years later led them to consent willingly to revising the role of the state. When the Keynesian fever of the seventies was followed by neoliberal uneasiness in the face of top-heavy bureaucracy, and people sought to reduce the size, budgets, and programs of the state, the forty-year-olds of the lyric generation, once partisans — and principal beneficiaries — of all-out interventionism were the first to "understand" the necessity for a change of direction in the interests of the common good. It must be said that these same forty-year-olds were then at the peak of their careers, which made them inordinately sensitive to the "scandalously" elevated level of fiscal spending, which had to be reduced to more "reasonable" proportions so it would not become "socially and economically counterproductive." In addition, since they had long passed the age when they would have to seek employment, the fact that the public and parapublic sectors were no longer recruiting had no effect on them. Those among them who had begun working for the state ten years earlier, when it was in full expansion, were either sheltered from any insecurity and entrenched in the

impregnable fortress of their "seniority," or were in adminis-
trative positions, always the last to disappear; in any case,
would managers complain if there were fewer young people
breathing down their necks?

As for those in private enterprise, they would of course
be the most radical proponents of "deregulation" and a
"smaller role" for the state. The very people who profited
more than anyone else from government involvement to carve
out a place for themselves in the economic establishment,
would be the first, once they had achieved their goals, to
denounce a cancerous, ineffective, "gluttonous" state. While
most of their "empires" would have been swallowed up in no
time and their "success stories" would have been only pipe
dreams without the timely backing of this or that law or
without the direct support of a government determined to
intervene on their behalf, now they were prepared to preach
entrepreneurship and propose that their fellow citizens learn
to compete on the open market instead of relying on public
intervention. They did not go so far, of course, as to demand
the abolition of the state, or even a return to the minimal
governance of classical liberalism. Rather, what they wanted
was a reorientation, a rejigging of the state that would result
in its abandoning or limiting its costly and unproductive
measures in favour of those that, according to them, were
relevant to the true touchstones of collective well-being:
technological competitiveness, the expansion of markets, the
availability of capital — the shoring up of their own empires
and the enhancement of their freedom of action.

Progress, in 1975, required action by the state. Progress,
in 1985, required its cessation. Always, what was expected of
the state was presented by those with power and authority as
a way of ensuring not only their own well-being, or the

reinforcement of their power, but prosperity and advancement for society itself, in other words, for all citizens, without any distinction based on age or condition. For such is the good fortune of the masters of the world: the grounds and the meaning of history may seem to change, but invariably they coincide with their own logic and their own intentions.

COLLABORATORS WITH MODERNITY

I have dwelt for some time on the recent evolution of government action in Quebec because it provides a clear illustration of the lyric generation's stranglehold on society in its adult years. But the evidence for such a shift in stewardship and its repercussions went far beyond the field of public administration — as might be expected. Some of it took the form of new doctrine, new programs of thought and action, new political, aesthetic, or moral ideas, all of which abounded during the seventies and gave free and open expression to the sensibility of this generation. Of all the outward signs of its new authority, these were certainly the easiest to observe and analyze, and that, of course, has been done at great length.

But candid and conspicuous as they were, the products of lyric ideology (to which I will return in due course) were only the offshoots of more important phenomena, through which this generation exerted its influence. What the new adults embodied was not so much a different way of looking at or thinking about the world, but a new way of living in it and comporting themselves in accordance with it. Everything was affected by what was in the air: not only politics and culture, but all of life in society and the very basis of existence.

All this makes an assessment difficult. For in order to reach a good understanding of the nature and the scope of these changes, we would have to be able to plumb a level so intimate and so profound that we would be dealing more with instinct than with thought, and would thus be compelled, in order to have anything to say at all, to confine ourselves to what is obscure, felt, and unarticulated. We would have to see, in short, that which conditions our way of seeing, to reflect on that which makes us reflect as we do. If only we could distance ourselves enough. But this ethos has made us what we are today, and the changes it has wrought have shrouded the old world in forgetfulness, so that it has become practically impossible for us to perceive what has changed; the world and the life we see are perfectly normal to us. How to find the vantage point from which to describe something, when that something is present everywhere we look? And so, any representation can only be approximate, indirect, and cloaked in hypotheses that are both cautious and incomplete.

My own hypothesis would go more or less as follows. The onset of adulthood for the firstborn of the baby-boom generation represented the ultimate triumph for what we know as *modernity*. Were it not for the control the lyric generation was able to exert over our times, the "modern" would never have succeeded so completely or so rapidly in taking possession of our world and our lives.

The terms of this hypothesis, of course, must be defined. First of all, what is "modern" and what is "modernity"? These words belong to a large family of much-parroted terms whose meaning changes at will, depending on who is speaking and what is being spoken about. For the purposes of my own analysis, they depict the present world not as it breaks with tradition, but as it knows itself to be, and wants itself to be, the locus of such a rupture. What would be modern in these terms is not so much that which is distinct from the old, but that which cultivates this distinction and pursues it for its own sake as an intrinsic good that is beyond discussion and has no reference to anything else. Modernity, thus conceived, would not be defined in terms of this or that attribute, but rather as an ingrained mistrust of anything stable or inherited and the constant quest for the new.

That understood, it seems to me that we can isolate two contrasting perspectives from which the idea of the modern may be viewed. The first is a negative or polemical perspective, according to which the modern would be defined in terms of the rejection of everything that would presume to subordinate the individual or the community to something — a source, a norm, a goal — "superior," "foreign," or inaccessible to it. Modernity, from this point of view, would rule out anything that limits, regiments, and depreciates current existence in the name of some authority, constancy, or meaning imposed from outside: myth, divinity, transcendence, the past, authority itself. The modern would thus evolve as an ongoing process of liberation and transgression, leading to the eventual decline of all values and practices liable to hem the individual in and have him comply with wishes or intentions not entirely his own. To be modern would imply a struggle that would never end, with criticism and denial being the weapons of choice.

The other view of what is modern represents the positive side of the coin. It glorifies this same criticism and denial: the euphoria attached to what is new and current, faith in what is emerging rather than what endures, pleasure in knowing no limit or horizon other than one's own will and one's own powers, here and now. The modern individual, from this perspective, would be happy because he is a liberated carefree person with no memories to weigh him down. He will have

made his home in that *empire of the ephemeral* so well described by the French sociologist Gilles Lipovetsky.

This dual definition is based on one proposed by Hans
Robert Jauss to account for the modern conception of modernity: its meaning is to be found in the antithesis — I would
add, the antagonism — that opposes it to the idea of *eternity*.
The modern, for us, is both the denial and denunciation of
the eternal (the negative perspective) and the happy immer-
sion (positive perspective) in what Baudelaire called "the
transitory, the fugitive, the contingent," a territory of pure
instability and perpetual destruction followed by perpetual
renewal, and yet the only territory, in our view, with any
credibility or ontological substance.

According to Jauss, this conception assumed its final form
in Western literary and philosophical consciousness in the
second half of the nineteenth century. This does not mean
that the phenomenon of modernization thus understood —
the dethronement of the eternal in favour of the power and
beauty of what is now — did not begin much earlier in history
to modify the relationship between the individual and the
world, between one individual and another, between the
individual and himself, if only as a result of the development
of scientific thought and the decline of religion. But until
Baudelaire and Nietzsche this movement went relatively unnoticed, barely penetrating the collective consciousness. And
it would continue to go unnoticed for some time yet, outside
the realms of art and philosophy and the social milieu that
fostered them. It is easy to say that as of the end of the
nineteenth century the modernist ideal would occupy a privileged place in philosophical and aesthetic thought, and
would even determine their development; but the fact remains that this ideal, for most of our century, would be
confined to that sphere alone. Even within it, its propositions

would for a long time be largely polemic, associated as they were with extremely small circles of the avant-garde. In short, modern consciousness and sensibility might well have shaken up thought and culture, but they had little effect on daily life or immediate experience. The same thing could be said with respect to the other meaning of modernization, which denotes the evolution of socioeconomic structures (industrialization, urbanization) and progress in science and technology. Even though the process had begun in the nineteenth century, its effects on lifestyles and thinking remained superficial for a very long time. There remained such a temporal and mental gap between technological "conquest" and the rearrangement of social and economic organization on the one hand, and daily life on the other, that innovation, progress, and change had little impact on ordinary consciousness and the normal routine of individual and social life. They continued to be viewed and evaluated in terms of archaic norms based essentially on the permanence of traditions and the stability of the world. Modernization was a distant and abstract phenomenon and, as such, virtually invisible to the naked eye. Certainly, whatever was modern had its fascination, and modern innovations elicited admiration and envy. But this sense of wonder derived in large part from their strangeness, their unimaginable (or unimagined) dimension, and their remoteness from life and the world as perceived and experienced at the time.

In our century, however, and in particular since the Second World War, the process entered a new phase, distinguished by an unprecedented acceleration in changes of all sorts linked to this same modernization. The changes became so constant, so general, and so rapid, and they took such diverse forms and touched on so many aspects of reality, that day-to-day life and immediate experience were not only increasingly affected, but were swept up in the process and could no longer be regarded as areas of stability, calm, and imperturbable continuity. The modern became familiar, and it was the immemorial and the eternal that were receding from life.

This insinuation of the modern into daily life, and the moral revolution that followed, at first met with some resistance, as observed, for example, in the society of the fifties, and even the beginning of the sixties. However committed society was to this mutation, it was still strongly attached to traditional values, or to their forms and doctrines at the very least, and it continued to make reference to "what has always been," whether in religion, history, humanity, or the nature of things. Modernization may have permeated life and totally altered its rhythm and character, but people's *sense of life* was still informed by the past. Even a city dweller or the owner of a car and a television set in 1955 could, for the most part, have understood the language of the average adult a century earlier and could have adhered to his values and shared his sensibility. Modernization met its last resistance in a residual feeling for life wherein subsisted, however diminished, however frail, however abashed at times, the memory of an older world, the world that had always been there.

When I say — to return to my initial hypothesis — that the lyric generation's assumption of adulthood marked the final victory of modernity and that it made possible this victory, I am referring especially to the melting away of this last resistance, the final refuge of the "premodern." This generation was the first to identify itself with and to *consent* with all its heart to the process of modernization, to make the entrenchment of the modern and the eradication of everything opposed to it the very crux of its existence and its mission in the world. Thanks to the lyric generation, to the control and the authority that were now its own, the last moorings gave way, and the eternal, in people's hearts, as well as in ideology and institutions, departed definitively from this life, so that perpetual renewal and the ephemeral might reign supreme everywhere, with not a single pocket of resistance. In this respect, we could say that one of the historical roles of the lyric generation was to make itself the instrument — or to cite another expression of Milan Kundera, the devoted *collaborator* — of modernity. Or again, we could say that modernity was the outward sign of the lyric generation's sway over the world.

Their collaboration and identification with the modern reflected the fact that the sensibility and expectations this generation evolved in their youth were imported intact into a maturity that far from tempering them, reinforced and enhanced their power. And they reflected exactly that denial of the eternal and infatuation with novelty for its own sake that are the key to my own definition of modern consciousness. It is a consciousness that up till then had remained marginal and rather avant-garde, but that with this generation became the normal way of understanding and evaluating individual and social life. Any hint of the old Parmenidean mentality, centred on conservation and permanence, had been eliminated, to be replaced by the new Heraclitean ethos of constant movement, renewal, and infinite lightness.

But the lyric generation also collaborated with modernity in that it was in perfect accord with the world as shaped by the modernization process that constantly broke it down, only to rebuild it. The transitory, fugitive, and contingent effects of capitalism's advance and technological "triumphs" were viewed not as an accident remote from the centre of life, but as its natural element, its home, and no feelings of strangeness or nostalgia were experienced. The new was its entire kingdom, and beyond its borders all was silent and deserted.

The lyric generation did not *invent* modern sensibility or consciousness any more than its accession to adulthood *caused* modernization. The latter had been in the works for a very long time and would have eventually triumphed regardless. It would be more appropriate — to quote what Tocqueville said of the French Revolution in 1789 — to say that the lyric generation "suddenly achieved . . . with no transition, precautions, or forethought, what would have been accomplished little by little on its own in the long run." Invested since childhood and youth with an irrepressible longing for rupture that was totally compatible with the modern project, the lyric generation, from the moment it assumed control of the world, took it upon itself to sweep away in one stroke anything that might have hindered or delayed the project's realization. The lyric generation's role thus consisted not so much in provoking as in facilitating and accelerating modernization, and the very existence of this multitude committed to rupture and new beginnings offered the most favourable conditions for its rapid dissemination and final victory over the world and our minds.

My hypothesis, if it is valid, therefore suggests that modernity, a complex phenomenon if ever there was one, aside from its philosophical, technological, and socioeconomic foundations, also had as a support, or supplementary component, this disturbance of the demographic equilibrium represented by the explosion of the lyric generation and the baby boom. In abruptly altering the relationship between generations, in stripping the older generation of their secular authority and curtailing if not actually doing away with their moderating influence on the evolution of ideas and customs, this disturbance gave free rein to the circulation of the forms and content of modernity, now legitimized and fully authenticated by their association with a confident new generation whose ethos and desires were gaining strength, unchecked by any delay or compromise.

I know that such a hypothesis is not easy to verify. In conclusion, I will restate the only argument I have of any substance: the observed *agreement* between our modernity, which generated the newness and spirit of our times, and what I consider the genius of the lyric generation. This agreement has been so complete, it seems to me, and modernity *suited* the lyric generation so perfectly, has brought it so much happiness, has so faithfully answered its expectations, and so exactly articulated its view of the world and life that one might very well say modernity was the object of the lyric generation's desire and the product of its actions.

THE LYRIC IDEOLOGIES

One of the principal contributions of the lyric generation to contemporary history remains the astonishing abundance of arguments, doctrines, ideas, and programs of all sorts that its accession to adulthood brought about. No other generation has exercised in such striking manner the freedom of thought and expression it derived from being admitted to public life, and none has produced or consumed as many ideals, slogans, and theories; none has been so fascinated by ideology and the word or dedicated itself to them with as much zeal.

This growth peaked during the seventies and early eighties, and greatly contributed to the notoriety of those years as a period of transition, characterized by a general crisis in values. What is certain is that it was a time like no other for "societal projects," "epistemological leaps," "paradigm changes," and other speculative cataclysms. In our memories, the period still resonates with a certain Babelian excitement.

Among the reasons for such discursive bulimia, there was first of all the fact that, compared with others, the lyric generation went to school for a very long time. It therefore produced an appreciable contingent of intellectuals, academics, artists, writers, editorialists, researchers, union officials, specialists in the social sciences, publishers of reviews, authors of manifestos, and other opinion makers, all in safe professions respected by the press and television. Where Quebec was concerned, we could even say with very little exaggeration that what we call the intelligentsia, that is, a milieu concerned entirely with words and ideas, was an invention of this generation. As of the seventies, the intelligentsia was so monopolized and "colonized" it that it was turned into an institution far more visible and vibrant than had been the case in the past, and thus was made into one of the lyric generation's most privileged organs.

But no intelligentsia can survive if it is not listened to. And there again, the adults of the lyric generation, thanks to their level of education and preoccupation with always being of their time, formed a particularly interested and receptive public. The habits they had acquired at college and university had familiarized them with the world of ideas and convinced them of the need constantly to renew them, to push them ever further, and to accept, even to encourage, the advancement of intellectual progress. Their hunger for new ideas, unprecedented points of view, and audacious arguments created a demand for ideology that was stronger than ever and a climate that could not have been more conducive to the burgeoning of doctrines and their wide circulation.

In addition, this public was large in number, influential, generally well off, and had the leisure and the means to indulge its passion. In *La mirage linguistic* (*The Linguistic Mirage*), Thomas Pavel of Princeton University noted that there was in the exaggerated thirst for ideology and what one might call the frenzy for theoretical innovation something that smacked of "discretionary social behaviour," that is, a kind of diversion or luxury available only to those with a surplus of material and intellectual resources that could be consumed or squandered, even at a loss, for there were, strictly speaking, no consequences to fear. Although all the ideological ferment of the decade cannot be reduced to such a mechanism, it remains, nevertheless, that there was a strong element of frivolity, answering less to the objective urgency of situations than to the need for intellectual stimulation that the rich require so as not to succumb to ennui. That, at least, is an explanation difficult to dismiss if one wants to understand some of the more exorbitant propositions of the time and, especially, to fathom how they could have been put forward and embraced with a seriousness we today would find disconcerting were it not for our recognizing that such behaviour was inspired by a taste for low-risk adventure and what I would call an ideological thrill.

That said, for the most part this period abounded in good faith and sincerity. Also, perhaps, naivety. In any case, a zeal to rethink the world has hardly been seen since and will doubtless not be seen for some time. There one may discern, I think, besides the misappropriation of the immense reserve of ideas to which the lyric generation had access, another sign of the eternal youth that was its legacy. These radical thinkers, these liberators of peoples, these assassins of traditions, these enlargers of consciousness, these stealers of fire may well have been over thirty, but they retained all the freshness and generosity of their adolescent souls. To them the world continued to appear infinitely light and malleable, open to any and all transformations, and always willing to be destroyed and rebuilt on entirely new foundations. One had only to desire something, and reality obeyed. In this respect, these years were indeed a simple extension of what went before. It was the same mood, the same fever, the same lyricism. Except that what in the past sprang from an instinctive discontent, a rebellion without a cause, was now expressed in reasoning, theories, and well-articulated ideological platforms, which were to these adults what rock had been to the young people they had been not so long ago: a means of setting themselves apart and recognizing one another, a sign of their election and of their vocation in the world.

That is why, ten or fifteen years later, even though the ideological passion has dulled and the utopias of this feverish period have been forsaken by the very people who had preached their virtues most zealously, the lyric generation continues to see itself as faithful, in its fashion, if not to the ideas that it defended, at least to the desires that inspired them. Just as the lyric generation has remained committed to rock music as the sound that was central to its identity, so this generation continues to harbour an interest for apocalyptic discourse and promises of salvation. Its members no longer believe in them, of course, but they cannot help but lend them an ear as if to an echo of a better part of themselves, alas now vanished. They retain, in short, the ideological reflex and its habit, its *shape*.

To return to this period of great intellectual luxury, it is impossible to compile an inventory of ideas and programs to which the lyric generation gave its support. We will content ourselves with a necessarily incomplete typology, which will at least have the merit of being brief. It will divide the representative ideologies of this generation (understood: whose principal advocates were recruited from its ranks and that experienced their greatest success among its members) into three broad categories, according to what field, or target, they favoured.

First of all, there were the *societal* ideologies, the most important of which was Marxism with its multiple variants, including Third-World ideologies, the aim of which was to overthrow capitalism and the socioeconomic bourgeois order and to install either a new power founded on the proletariat or a society in which all power relationships would have disappeared. I am leaving aside Quebec nationalism for the moment, which was not a typical product of this generation. Next came the ideologies of the *self*, all derived, more or less, from Freudian theory laced with Eastern mysticism imported from California. It advocated the total emancipation of the individual and the full flowering of his faculties, through mental and dietetic asceticism, the unblocking of residual sexual inhibitions, psychedelic experiments, "listening" to oneself, and the patient, methodical exploration of the body's vast precincts, consciousness, and the intimate. The principal function of these ideologies was to justify the moral freedom that these adults had known since they were young and that unlike young people before them, they had not had to renounce as they grew older. And so hedonism, paradoxically, became an enterprise obeying the decrees of reason and pursuing ends with a theoretical grounding.

The contrast between societal ideologies and ideologies of the self could not have been greater, at least on the level of principles. In fact, however, they were far from being as antagonistic as one might think. It was not unusual, towards the end of the seventies, to encounter rather curious hybrids: a reincarnationist communist talking with a vegetarian Trotskyite, a Zen Maoist well versed in the writings of the Marquis de Sade, or a disciple of transcendental meditation who swore only by the Albania of Enver Hoxha. For the lyric mentality, rigour and the principle of contradiction were of secondary importance; they were regarded as constraints, as vestiges of bourgeois and humanist "logocentrism," which had to be abandoned if individuals wanted to think freely and in harmony with the requirements of the period of mutation in which they had the good fortune to live. What counted was not the coherence of thought, but openness, authenticity, and the courage of commitment.

The frequent confusion between these first two categories of ideology may also be explained by the lyric generation's special brand of apprenticeship — or nonapprenticeship. Never having been required to deal with the notion that the world was separate from them, lyric individuals naturally tended to project their own existence and identity onto the outside world, and to internalize the world as though it were part of their private life. Any personal problem immediately became a problem for society, and vice versa, so that revolution would mean both changing oneself and changing the system. "Expanding one's mind" through drugs or collective lovemaking had as much political significance for the lyric personality as participating in a strike or founding a terrorist cell. "To remake life, to rebuild the world: it is the same project," preached Vaneigem's *Treatise*.

That said, in the seventies and the beginning of the eighties the two ideologies did not have the same status. Those that concerned society, after having peaked around 1970–75, quickly went into decline; they appeared less and less fertile and stirring, while the ideologies of the self took advantage of the vacuum thus created and increased enormously in popularity. This can be shown by following the "itineraries" of a large number of the most popular thinkers of this generation, who moved almost without transition from upholding the most impersonal scientific and radical social and political activism to defending no less passionately the new values and total fulfilment for the individual, moved from unions to ashrams, from the workers' revolution to the sexual revolution, from political manifestos to magic mushrooms. This ideological evolution, this abandonment of societal projects in favour of the quest for and exaltation of the self, may be seen as another indication of the lyric generation's growing control over the world around it, a world it no longer needed, as a result, to rethink from beginning to end. Since society obeyed and reflected the lyric generation more and more, why would one want to transform it?

But the richest ideological cocktails may be found in my third category. Positioned as it was midway between the other two, it borrowed its "models" and references sometimes from one and sometimes from the other, but most often from both at once. This last category groups together what I call ideologies of *culture,* which addressed the status, nature, and meaning of the intellectual and symbolic universe, and the activities that came within its ken. The times teemed with these ideologies. In writings on literature, the visual arts, theatre, cinema, and other cultural disciplines, there was an endless succession of theoretical "breakthroughs," "callings into question," and decisive "ruptures." A new school of thought, a new aesthetic approach, or a new language had no sooner seen the light of day than it was immediately criticized, demystified, and replaced by yet another that was more advanced, more contemporary.

I am not thinking so much here of published works, although it goes without saying that that torrent of words had its effect, as I am of the abundance of programs, manifestos, "grids," "approaches" — the whole conceptual sideshow — that accompanied, preceded, and weighed down their existence and that of works from the past — in short, all of cultural life. The variety of interpretations, or "readings," would dishearten the most long-suffering cataloguer.

If culture experienced such an ideological explosion and was the battleground for such prolonged debates, it was in part due to the ease with which it could be discussed. It was, in other words, the perfect terrain for the aforementioned discretionary behaviour. While the societal ideologies had sooner or later to deal with reality, were it only to denounce or destabilize it, and while the ideologies of the self promised results for which to some degree they could be held accountable, what set the cultural ideologies apart was that they were immune to and even refused any sort of verification whatsoever, to the point where they could literally say *anything at all*. A theory of art or a definition of culture was never rejected because of its inadequacy or lack of validity, or because the "reality" had changed. What killed it was always its own decline, its redundancy, the weakening of its own impact, which derived from one source alone: its novelty. However indispensable, however vital cultural ideologies may have seemed when they first appeared, they were destined to vanish not long afterwards to make way for opposing ideologies, until the latter declined in turn, and the former were rediscovered and seen in a new light. What was important was that there be ideas, discourse, and noise.

It will not have gone unnoticed that in my little typology there is a surprising omission: feminism. It is not that I consider the issue unimportant. I regard it as *the* great ideology of the period, the strongest expression of the new spirit and the new mentality fostered by the lyric generation. But feminism — or more precisely, the neofeminism or radical feminism that developed over these years and whose ideas were disseminated largely within the intelligentsia — was, as a theory, too all-encompassing to be absorbed by any of my three categories. It was neither a societal ideology, nor one of the self, nor one of culture, but all of them at once. And so one saw feminists, both men and women, sometimes advocating social revolution (and forging purely tactical alliances with the Marxists), sometimes sexual revolution (and joining forces with the adherents of self-liberation), and sometimes the revolution of language and aesthetic codes. It was on this last front of symbols and culture that feminism knew its greatest success, perhaps for the reasons I elucidated earlier. But whatever the target, the project and vision remained the same: to unmask and denounce the secular "phallocracy," to put an end to it, and to transform completely the relationships between the sexes.

It is unfair, I know, to schematize as I have done the ideological life of this period, but it at least makes it possible to identify its principal features: profusion, diversity, and intensity. I would like to focus on two or three other characteristics common to the schools of thought I have singled out, which provided intellectual nourishment for the most educated of the lyric generation.

The first is the lack, if not the total absence, of originality. There was hardly a single *ideology* whose content was not in one way or another the reworking or echo of a *system of thought* conceived and expressed earlier in the century, under conditions and in contexts that were often very different. Where society, the self, or culture were concerned, the fiery arguments of the seventies and eighties proposed virtually no new ideas, no theory that went beyond or that truly distinguished itself from the modern intellectual and artistic tradition, that is, ideas and theories that had been current in even moderately innovative circles in Europe or the United States since the end of the nineteenth century, and that had been the object, since the Second World War especially, of assessments and reformulations that greatly contributed to their wider dissemination. The discourse of the lyric generation, in that respect, was essentially a borrowed and mimetic discourse, which repeated words that had already been pronounced, and freely spent conceptual capital that had been stored up by its predecessors long before. It was a discourse of epigones.

Of course, there is no such thing as pure originality, and every school of thought is nourished by its antecedents, for it is the very essence of thought — and of culture — to draw on what came before it. But in the case of the lyric generation, the dependence was such that rather than stimulating, supporting, or inspiring research and reflection, it put an end to them before they could even begin. The master, the guru, was for the epigone a source of answers, not of questions; he offered certainty and enthusiasm, not perplexity. It was not admiration or emulation that bound the epigone to the master, but identification and awestruck obedience, much like the relationship between the rock-music public and its idols.

To see these repetitive thought processes at work, one need only leaf through some of the more so-called revolutionary texts or reviews of the time. The "postulates" invariably give rise to "corollaries," the "references" to "restatements," the arguments from authority to the begging of questions, the "accepted conclusions" to the "facts already established." From page to page, from paragraph to paragraph, the same formulas recur, like incantations: "It has now been shown that . . ." or "As X has demonstrated . . ." or "It follows from this that . . ." or "Whoever has read Y knows that . . ." All this was accompanied by a constant, obsessive, truly incantatory bombardment of quotations: Artaud, Althusser, Aurobindo, Barthes, Breton, Brecht, Engels, Foucault, Gramsci, Jung, Lacan, Marcuse, Reich, Sartre/de Beauvoir, among others.

In other words, the newness so proudly proclaimed by the lyric ideologies at the time was entirely relative: new, doubtless, if set beside the thoughts and beliefs of these educated adults' parents and grandparents; new in respect to the peremptory tone and rhetoric of terrorism employed by their expositors, as well; but certainly not new in content, since none of them, in truth, invented anything at all in

conceptual terms. These ideologies, as well as the arguments
that conveyed them and the conduct they inspired, were all
typical of what I would call a *neo*-mentality, the prefix not
meaning the same thing as "new."

What distinguished neo-Marxism, neofeminism, neo-
Freudianism, and the other neoideologies was their hardening
and systematization of the source-theory and its transformation into *evidence*. Once that was accomplished, the work of
the neothinker, aside from the accumulation of glosses that
supposedly confirmed the revealed truth, was to restate the
dogma, disseminate it, and widen its sphere of application,
gilding the lily, so to speak. Saussure had postulated that the
link between sign and sense was arbitrary; the neo-Saussurian
concluded that the sign had no connection with the sense.
Rimbaud, who was an avant-garde writer, had written in one
of his poems: "We must be absolutely modern"; the neo-
avant-gardist concluded that everything published before
1970 was outdated. Marx had seen in the class struggle the
way to justice and equality; the neo-Marxist concluded that
one had to wage battle alongside bureaucrats and educators
against the domination of the bourgeois state. Reformist
feminists in the past had denounced the political, legal, and
economic inferiority of women; the neofeminist demanded
that woman writers be studied only by writers of the same sex,
or refused to let little boys play with tin soldiers. What was
"new" in the neoapproach, was the overkill.

If the lyric ideologies invented little, they destroyed
much, verbally at least, for here we are concerned primarily
with arguments and words. One of the characteristic attitudes
of many intellectuals of this generation, and therefore a
common feature of the three broad categories of ideology
referred to earlier, was what I would call an obsession with the
end. Whether it was a matter of the organization of society,

the conduct of the individual, or the state of culture, the basic principle on which any theoretical analysis was founded was that things, as they are and as they were, constituted both an error that had to be corrected and a vast fraud that had to be terminated. Even, and perhaps above all, when their declared aim was to work for the happiness and liberty of mankind, the social institutions, the culture, the religions, or the established moral systems were nothing more than instruments of oppression and alienation. The world, in short, was a usurpation that had gone on long enough. History had taken the wrong path, and we had to turn our backs on all that, burn our bridges, and move on to other things.

This obsession with, or desire for, the end resulted in two types of closely related ideological behaviour, although one, as we shall see, clearly dominated the other. One was prophetism, and the other, subversion. Prophetism was the contemplation and proclamation of, and at times the a priori experimentation with, the new world that had to and would replace our own. It was the Great Event, the universal reign of beauty and equality; it was poetry for and by everyone; it was body and soul together at last, free of all restraints; it was the transfiguration of consciousness and victory over death. All promises and all utopias were good.

For what counted was not so much the realization of a dream, but rather the grounds the dream provided for refusing that which was. Prophetism was subversion's justification, and its weapon. Subversion was the interdiction of anything representing order or values that had been handed down, imposed, or passed on, which would be subject either to systematic deconstruction, or to challenges and violations that were no less systematic. The most striking feature of lyric thought was what some called its nonconformism, that is, its eagerness to mistrust and reject everything that came before it and laid claim to "the truth." Despite, or perhaps because of, the lyric generation's enthusiasm for the paradise to come, whose imminent arrival it deemed certain, it was profoundly disenchanted with reality. This generation's hopes for a new world justified working for the ruin of the world around it and from which it had withdrawn its allegiance.

Nothing better illustrates this frenzy of devastation than the cultural ideologies prevalent during the seventies, in what was then called the "counterculture," an amalgam of heterogeneous currents of thought, all of which asserted (1) that Western culture in general was a fraud that had to be opposed through the glorification of everything it had forbidden or repressed up to then: the Dionysiac, the popular, the deviant, the play-oriented, any minority phenomenon; and (2) that culture itself, as a way of relating to the world, was like morality and power: it was an obstacle, a trap, and therefore it was vital to put an end to it by demystifying it, "disintellectualizing" the spontaneous "creativity" of individuals. Art, thought, and poetry were to be found neither in museums nor in books; they were in the street, in Bob Dylan's songs, in LSD-induced "trips," and in the joyous innocence of "real-life" experience. True culture, the only culture that was "authentic" and liberating, was the opposite of traditional culture. It was its subversion, its depreciation, its absence.

When we try today to balance the books of the counterculture, where quality is concerned, we find that the "credit" column, that is, of new works that it produced and theoretical advances that it made, seems quite unimpressive. On the other hand, the negative accomplishments of the counterculture have been considerable; we remain very much in its debt for the trivialization and devaluing of intellectual and cultural activity, which is one of the most striking features of our modernity.

During the seventies, the influence of the lyric ideologies was most in evidence in the field of literature. At a time when the public was more numerous and more enthusiastic than ever, when literature seemed finally to have freed itself from censorship and from the commissioned work that had for so long hemmed it in, when government support for writing, publishing, and reading was becoming increasingly effective, at a time, in short, when everything seemed in place to make possible a "normal" literary life, lo and behold, a vast theoretical and ideological offensive was launched against the lies and misdeeds of literature.

One might have expected that these attacks would have come from the outside, that they would have been the work of various ideological entities and powers that felt themselves threatened by the liberating effect of books and who sought to strip them of prestige and influence. But no, it was at the very hub of what one had begun to call the literary establishment that these accusations were conceived and that a systematic campaign of sabotage was initiated, which would not end until it had decisively turned literature against itself, in the words of Gerald Graff, and had bled it of all its legitimacy and relevance.

The professional critics and educators, first of all, set themselves the task of exposing on the one hand the purely conventional, or anodyne, character of literary works and genres, and on the other the imposture of authors, who only masked beneath agreeable aesthetic affectations their class prejudices and a host of unavowed presuppositions. Or again, they "demonstrated" how literature was elitist and cut off from real life, how aesthetic values were a simple matter of circumstance and entrenched positions, and how books had nothing true to say about the world. In short, it was a question of dethroning the old humanist idol, of demystifying it; of disabusing the reader and the writer by "freeing" them from literature and its charms. In Quebec, this operation was also an occasion to discredit, at little cost, those authors and critics who still retained some lingering esteem or residual admiration for French literature, which was, after all, just one literature among many. It was just a bit more snobbish, a bit more disconnected, and a bit more universal, and therefore much more "imperialist" than the others.

In this enterprise, the writers themselves, those of the new generation in particular, were not to be outdone. It was the golden age of "new writing," a catchall category that grouped together all those whose aim was to do away with the forms and codes of Western literature. Even the very word *literature* was to be avoided, as it was far too pregnant with bourgeois and idealist connotations. One had to talk of "writing," of "production," of "signifying practices" resulting in "texts" (not works) that were "semiotic structures" whose primary function was to "operate displacements," to "explode the limits" of language and meaning by "inscribing" or "speaking" the body in their "discourse." In reality, only one thing counted: to write against literature, to write unimpeded by the old myths (old demands), embodied in literary tradition. This is what was called taking a plunge into the unknown, taking risks, accepting the rupture. And the writers who did so were considered, and considered themselves, heros.

Whether it expressed itself in literature or elsewhere, this passion for innovation was certainly one of the trademarks of the times, and it is the reason that era still inspires so much nostalgia in those who took part in it. To innovate, then, was to start over from scratch, to refuse to pursue what was already under way and so to make a clean slate. All that the thinkers of the lyric generation were inclined to retain of the past, and of the writings and ideas of those who came before, was what directly served their cause: the reasoning, concepts, and theoretical support that would arm them against the world of their parents and teachers. Aside from that, the past was an enemy to bring down. All they conserved of the past, therefore, was the idea, the myth of the avant-garde. In their view, there was no viable thought or action that did not make a break, transgress, or reject the rule of law and go beyond. Everything was measured according to this standard. Whether it was a matter of political theory or strategy, morals, art or literature, or even types of computers or culinary techniques, nothing that did not transcend, did not exceed some limit, or was not audacious had any merit. On this point there was consensus, and one might say that the lyric ideology, in whatever field it found expression, represented a wholehearted endorsement of the avant-garde point of view, which determined the one way of thinking and of acting that deserved respect.

Clearly, this was a unique situation, and one not without its ironies. Like everything associated with the lyric generation, the triumph of the ideas and attitudes of the avant-garde was, among intellectuals, artists, writers, and their public, such a massive and generalized phenomenon, and one so easily achieved, that it lost all its heroic character, all its weight, and ultimately, all significant meaning. For what is an avant-garde if it is no longer in the minority? How is it possible to be or to remain avant-garde when the avant-garde has become the norm?

Certainly, traditionally and by definition, every avant-garde was a group phenomenon: the encyclopaedists, the romanticists, the impressionists, the futurists, the surrealists, and so on, up to the "neoplasticists." But these groups remained small minorities in the milieu where they sprang up, a milieu that they contested and wanted to transform, certainly, but that resisted their importunities and stood up to them, for a period of time at least. It was, in fact, this very resistance and this "period of time" that made these little groups the avant-garde.

That was not at all what occurred, of course, when avant-gardism, with which the artists and thinkers of the lyric generation instantly identified, established itself throughout the milieu where the new arrivals were deployed. That some of their elders, who were part of the avant-garde, closed ranks with them and welcomed them with open arms was not surprising. These elders were simply acknowledging their spiritual kinship with the newcomers and took advantage of the support they offered, as did the frustrated reformers in the sixties. Who, feeling unappreciated by his contemporaries, would not, like Stendhal, look forward to being recognized by his great-nephews? What is remarkable, rather, when one considers the arrival on the scene of the new avant-garde, is that practically all elders received it with the same enthusiasm, or goodwill at the very least, and, above all, that there were so few among them who dared swim against the current or oppose it with any conviction. The fact is that there was no longer any rear guard or establishment worthy of the name. Those who would normally have composed it were either too small in number or too unsure of what it was they had to defend, and too weak in any case to stand in the way of the newcomers. And so they were silent or, more frequently, saw the way the wind was blowing and adjusted accordingly. Once again the invasion, the ideological tide, met no true obstacle.

This is the source of the irony I referred to above. Obliged by their birth and education to remain true to themselves, "to be absolutely modern," to invent, advance, and always be daring while sweeping aside everything in their path, the new Rimbauds found nothing to overturn or bring down, neither the old who resembled the "leprous flowering on old walls," nor mother with her "blue gaze — that lies!" Everywhere the audience was rising to its feet or was already standing, and the mothers, far from damning them for their excesses, applauded them with all their hearts, when they were not themselves joining in the rebellion with all speed. What is the new when there is no longer any old? Or the modern when tradition no longer puts up a struggle?

There is something pathetic in this irony, for to lose the enemy is the worst thing that can happen to a militant. Sensing that his rebellion risks losing its edge for lack of an obstacle, he tends to turn it upon himself and to become its only victim. For example, the writer of *joual* becomes complacent or no longer writes when no one insists on the necessity of respecting the forms and structures of the written language. As for the avant-garde painter who proclaims "the end of the myth of art," while all around him colleagues, critics, museum curators, and gallery owners are either making the same demand or are honouring it as a fait accompli, he has two choices, if he still believes in his rebellion: one is to rebel against *art* and start painting chromos (this is the postmodern approach, in part); the other is to persist in loudly demanding what everyone has already agreed to, in other words, to succumb to academicism, which is often, today, the fate, in art and elsewhere, of the once subversive avant-garde.

Is that to say that the lyric ideologies failed? To answer this question, we must first ask ourselves what, really, was their project, what exactly was the "cause" they set out to serve. As I have said, these ideologies foretold all sorts of marvels: revolution, transformation, salvation, rebirth. None of these promises, in truth, was kept. Ten or fifteen years after the great upheavals and the penetrating arguments, we see today that all that was only words. Either the ideals have been forgotten, or they have been radically watered down. Despite "political correctness," a fashionable variation on the great revolutionary themes of yore, capitalism, conservatism, and economicism have never thrived so well. Yoga, drugs, transcendental meditation, and emancipated eroticism have become relaxation techniques that help executives in their forties to remain young, to perform better, and to make more money. Even in literature we are witnessing the rediscovery of "readability," a "return to realism," the trivialization of form and content, the "professionalization" of writers — in short, the undisputed triumph of the business mentality and the bourgeois conventions that were treated with such contempt in the recent past. All that has the consent, if not the active collaboration, of those who not long ago dedicated themselves heart and soul to overthrowing the established order and to starting history over again from the beginning.

This seeming failure of the lyric project obscures, however, what was in fact a great victory. The lyric generation did succeed through its ideological upheaval in obtaining what it most ardently desired: its own liberation and its own lightness, in other words, the extension and the legitimization of its power over the world. Under the guise of changing society, life, or culture, their subversion had no other goal, in reality, but to clear the decks and discredit the heritage of earlier generations, so that the new masters would not have to account for anything or assume any continuity. To break with the past or transgress was for them but a way to rid themselves of memory and anything else that blocked the horizon. Proclaiming themselves free of all allegiance to the past and denying the validity of any options that might have opposed their actions and their works, they made themselves invulnerable to any guilt or any constraint. In the end, they totally vanquished the heaviness of the world.

This interpretation might help us to understand how we

were able to make the transition so quickly and abruptly from a period so charged with debate, ideas, and doctrines, as were the seventies and the beginning of the eighties, to the current climate, marked by what some have called the "end of ideology." Clearly, this is not the end of all ideologies, on the contrary. But it is true that those who so impassioned the lyric generation ten or fifteen years ago, today seem extremely pale. Abandoned by their followers and unable to attract new ones, sometimes even held in contempt, the social revolution, the "new consciousness," the "new writing," and even feminist doctrine seem more and more like moribund schools of thought that may have retained their nobility, certainly, but show no signs of life.

Some attribute this disaffection to the indolence and realistic attitude of young people today. It would be more accurate to see it as the price to be paid for the success the lyric ideologies had in their time, and as proof of the effectiveness with which the lyric generation accomplished the true and unique task it was assigned: not to change or save the world, but to *disencumber* it. And in this respect, we may say that it succeeded beyond all expectations: not only were old idols overturned and ancient myths unmasked, but the very need for idols and myths ceased to be a factor. At last the sky and earth were purged of all spirits, unburdened of any weight, left as silent and empty as on the first morning of the world.

Such was the ultimate subversion.

POLITICS DOMESTICATED

If the modernizing effect occasioned by the lyric generation's assumption of adulthood was marked by a kind of overweening enthusiasm and heightening of certain tendencies and processes initiated earlier on, one area where these repercussions were especially noticeable was politics. I will confine myself to one example: Quebec, which is most familiar to me, but which I consider applicable, *mutatis mutandis,* to most countries that experienced the baby-boom effect, and were influenced by the lyric generation.

My thesis, once more, is that of *collaboration,* founded on the correspondence between the expectations, attitudes, and worldview inspired in the lyric generation by its history and its sense of itself, as well as recent developments affecting political ideas and attitudes in our society. It is a relationship that will enable us to understand the one through the other, to see in the one, if not the direct result, at least the faithful reflection of the other.

I have already, in an earlier chapter, drawn attention to the fact that this generation, once it attained political maturity, reaped the rewards of most policies and initiatives issuing from the state, which took upon itself the needs and concerns of the new adults and placed at their disposal the bulk of its resources and power, even its conscience.

But such an appropriation — for that is what it was — could not have come about had it not been made possible by our present notions regarding politics and the state, which is to say the relationship between our private and public lives as embodied in institutions and government apparatus, along with a certain logic and certain goals. Now this idea, or the modern conception of this idea, may well have been latent and exerting its subtle influence on the evolution of political structures and thought ever since the nineteenth century, and even more so since the Second World War. But it only came to reign supreme in Quebec at about the beginning of the seventies, the time when political activity and the way it would be defined fell increasingly into the hands of those born after the war. Once again, the role of the lyric generation was not to innovate or to make the break, but to collaborate in the accomplishment of this innovation and rupture, and to do so all the more easily because the process was in perfect accord with its own aspirations and needs.

This change may be summed up as the desanctification of politics and most especially of the state. In Quebec it took the state some time to develop a sense of its status and role in public life. Up to the fifties or sixties (aside, perhaps, from the interlude of the Second World War), it was the church, first and foremost, that was considered, and acted as, the guardian of French-Canadian identity and its will to survive. But since it held its power from on high and was itself accountable only to a higher power, the church did not incarnate this will and identity so much as it imposed them on the faithful, in the name of an authority that they recognized, certainly, but that they knew had not been placed there by themselves. They felt powerless before it, while the church was not responsible to them in any meaningful way. Outside the city of God, where everything had already been arranged, their own city was virtually nonexistent. The state, confined to the space allotted it by the church, was but a derivative, a secondary institution, the secular arm of the society's only truly legitimate representative. Certainly, in Quebec, parliament and responsible government had been in place for a long time, but in practice they functioned as in a preparliamentary society that saw no need to project a comprehensive vision of itself or to take collective action in any public domain other than religion, where parliaments have little to do. Politics, therefore, was generally shortsighted and of no great interest; eternity overwhelmed it.

One of the most significant contributions of the Quiet Revolution, or at least the initial phase of the Quiet Revolution, its most revolutionary contribution, in fact, was to make possible, or rather *reveal,* the emergence of what was then called "L'État du Québec": the "State of Quebec." What was important here, was not so much — at least not at first — the nationalist dimension, but the *political* implications. The decisive change was not simply that the Quebec government saw itself as acting and speaking out in defence of Quebec's interests; all governments had done that in the past, in their own way, as had the church. What was truly new was the very concept and practice of statehood, the fact that Quebec society was making room for a secular sphere at its very heart. There the organization and conduct of the nation would be freely discussed among the citizens themselves and decisions made in the name of all as an expression of their common will, their *public* will, on behalf not of each individual alone, but of society as a whole.

That is what made those years so memorable. The political order, freed from its traditional dependency, viewed itself and was viewed as the arena where the entire nation acted in concert and made its voice heard, and where, after due deliberation, its wishes were obeyed. When Quebec threw itself into large ventures such as the nationalization of electricity, the development of the Manicouagan, the reform of education and social services, the founding of the General Financing Corporation, the creation of the Ministry of Cultural Affairs, or the opening of Quebec delegations abroad, these "politics of grandeur," as they were called, were "grand," not in terms of content, which could be fairly banal, but because of the meaning society bestowed on them. The entire population felt it was involved in these accomplishments, felt it had played a role in what was achieved. The legitimacy and moral authority of the state, in other words, derived from the right vested in it by each citizen — even if he had voted against the party in power — to represent him, to be the locus of his public life, that is, of his participation and that of others in the construction of their common world, insofar as it was the world of all.

One might say, and of course it was said, that this promotion of the state simply resulted from a kind of mythological transference: what had formerly been accorded the church — the right to act in their name and to keep them in thrall — French Canadians now simply handed over to civil authority. But this interpretation obscures a very important difference: the liberal state that established itself over the years remained a strictly secular, lay institution. That, indeed, was its most remarkable quality. Citizens surrendered to it neither their souls nor their individual salvation; they gave over to it only a part of their power to act, that which bound them to their fellow citizens and could not achieve its ends outside the collective context of give-and-take and cooperation that the political order required. A broad context, doubtless, but one that was well defined. Besides, at this time and in this specific instance there was no sign of a cult or religion of the state, neither among the population nor its elected representatives. To compare the faith and the political attitudes of this era with fascism or totalitarianism, as would certain academic neothinkers and authors of union manifestos, to blithely characterize this state as being an exploiter and a vulgar boss, would be to talk nonsense, to refuse to see reality for what it was, so as not to compromise the lyric purity of one's ideology.

That said, when we compare the state of that time to what it has become today, it is true that political feeling had something about it that was mystical. Citizens did not see the state as, first and foremost, an instrument of power trying to trespass on their own. Rather, they considered it to be an extension or an enlargement of themselves and their own power. It was *their* state not only in that it belonged to them and owed them its existence, but because it represented their collective responsibility, which they did not discharge just by handing it over, but which they assumed through it — through the positions and the initiatives it took in their name and with their consent.

I am not claiming, of course, that everything was rosy, or that Quebec always showed itself worthy of the sentiment expressed above. But that sentiment was there — that of the seriousness and the humanity of political life, the feeling that politics enacted one of the fundamental principles of a free life: the individual's emancipation from the bondage of personal experience and private interests. In this respect, we may say that the state, the public domain, did indeed represent a kind of transcendence, an elevated plane, one that was profane, certainly, strictly circumscribed, and always provisional, but that nevertheless commanded respect and what we must acknowledge as devotion. Otherwise, it is hard to credit the sort of "civic" spirit that marked, whatever one may say, political conduct and debate in Quebec at that time. The signs were there not only in the party programs, in the declarations and actions of many leaders, and in the discussions of militants, journalists, and voters, but also in the example of many civil servants, teachers, and other state employees, for whom "public service" meant a commitment that went beyond — without going so far as to usurp it altogether — that which they accorded their own personal well-being and career plan.

That such a commitment has become inconceivable today, that it is more liable now to arouse in us feelings of irony and pity than understanding and respect, shows how much our view of the state and public life has changed, to what point it has been liberated and modernized since the lyric generation made its debut in the political arena. Its arrival, I repeat, was not necessarily the cause of this change, but it was certainly one of the factors that precipitated it, facilitated it, and made its accomplishment inevitable.

For there could not have been a wider gulf than that between the mythic conception of the state that I have just described and the view of it typically held by the lyric generation. As adversary of all authority and all things "elevated," which regarded as illegitimate all who claimed to still life's flow and to limit desire, how could this generation have agreed to surrender the smallest part of itself to what would not be, to what would no longer be, entirely itself?

Such was the nature of the state and political life as conceived and implemented by the parents and predecessors of the lyric generation at the time of the Quiet Revolution. It was a state and a breed of politics that one could qualify as "republican," to employ the vocabulary of Régis Debray, in the sense that it aspired to be an ideal representation of society as a whole. It was based on principles and on a conception of the citizen that were both abstract and generous; they were universal as well, in that their link to the private lives and immediate needs of each individual remained indirect and secondary. These principles and this conception appealed rather to the aspect of a person that enabled him to free himself from the particularities of his condition, whether they were social, economic, cultural, or demographic. It was in this sense that there was no distinction between citizens in terms of their value, and that their equality — despite and even bearing in mind their differences — could be both postulated and strived for.

Now, for the lyric generation, who were convinced that it was in their power to renew society so long as they remained true to themselves and distinct from all others, such a "dispossession" was unacceptable. To conform to the higher interests of the state, to blend into an idealized image of society as a whole, would be to submit to the outside world, to betray oneself, and to betray one's mission. In short, it would be to agree to be only one generation among others, since, from the point of view of the abstract state, citizens had no sex, no race, no religion, no wealth, and certainly no age. Under such conditions, the young making their entry into the community would become partners to their elders, their fellow citizens, their equals. Such were the political implications of apprenticeship, of access to the public domain. But for the lyric generation, this parity with older age groups, this dissolving of the self into an ageless collectivity, implied not only the loss of its own identity, but the surrendering of its power and its position of centrality that had been conferred on it by its visibility and its weight in numbers. And so, it was in the interests of this generation, if it did not want to disappear into the pluralistic amalgam of the community, to reject any "transcendental" concept of the state, as well as the "alienating" moral standards that went along with it.

To this generational survival instinct, as we might call it, was added the obsession with eternal youth, which also ruled out, for this generation, any sort of identification with a republican style of state. As the mandated representative of the highest will of the community, and answerable to all, not excluding those with little authority and power, the state was indeed an adult affair for those people whose task it was to watch over others' lives and to act, if need be, against their own personal or short-term interests in order to safeguard their public interests, which coincided always with the interests of those for whom they had assumed responsibility. And the lyric generation could not accept this requirement to weigh itself down, to lose sight of itself, to *age*. Those who, as minors, had profited so greatly from the state's actions on their behalf and from the devotion of those adults whose responsibility they were, once their own turn came to assume this same responsibility, could only suspect the state of oppressive manoeuvrings. Yet all the while they steered its resources and power in their direction, demanding that the public sector be reduced, in other words, that their own debts be cancelled and their adult obligations with regard to others be annulled. And so, eternal youth would have the eternal right to receive all and to give nothing back, the right to be absolved forever of what Péguy called, not the birthright, but the birth trust.

Before arriving at the "postmodern" conclusion that would strip the state of virtually all its legitimacy, and advocate its quasi disappearance, the modern process of "desanctification" and "deinvestiture" of the public sector went through a phase that resulted, paradoxically, in an unprecedented expansion of the state apparatus and a considerable widening of the responsibilities that devolved to it, thanks to the transformation of the republican state into a democratic state (to retain the terminology of Régis Debray), sometimes called the welfare state, and sometimes — more accurately — the management state. In my opinion, it would be a bit too facile to see in the new state, as it evolved in the Quebec of the seventies, the extension or simple enlargement of the "State of Quebec" that appeared at the beginning of the previous decade. Just because the directions taken by the former were already contained in some of the concerns of the latter, it does not mean there was no radical break between the two, affecting the ways in which they defined themselves and in which they justified their existence. This rupture, which was in no way restricted only to Quebec, was well described by Hannah Arendt. It involved, on the one hand, a desertion of that high ground that made the state a reflection of the public consciousness of individuals, a place where goals were made visible to them, which, being wider and less immediate than their personal interests, were nonetheless their *own* goals, derived from them and ruling a part of their lives, in short, specifically political goals. On the other hand, it involved an elevation to the rank of responsibilities accruing to the state of goals and concerns heretofore the property of "domestic" consciousness and the private domain. It was not simply a question of their elevation, but of their preeminence, their coming to embody the highest purposes of politics and state policy. The "desanctification" of the public will was essentially only the sanctification of the private will and private interests.

This dethroned state's role was no longer to represent the general will to live in a common world; rather its function was to serve those individuals who made up society so that they might attain as easily as possible the personal happiness that was their right. These individuals, in the view of authority as it was now understood, were no longer defined, nor did they define themselves, as citizens first, but as separate entities. Now "taxpayers," now "beneficiaries," they formed a sort of clientele for which the state had to fulfil various private and daily needs, beginning and often ending with economic needs, which are by definition never satisfied. This ultramodern state thus became a vast service enterprise, which, to respond to the demands for well-being from its protégés, had constantly to take into consideration their specific circumstances. They were sometimes consumers, sometimes property owners, sometimes people with cars; they were sometimes women, sometimes young people, sometimes workers or their employers. And so, political authority, renouncing all claim to being a superior venue, where citizens gathered in public view to debate community affairs, became no more than the public projection of private matters, a kind of extended family — "the national household," as Hannah Arendt put it — whose only concerns were those of the average family unit: the budget first, then health, food, the furniture, how to fill leisure time. Its purpose was no longer to enable people to transcend themselves, to offer them a means to give expression to and put into practice their civic consciousness, but rather to comfort them and help them erase the memory of this consciousness, which might threaten their pursuit of private happiness.

Because it was dedicated to "social justice" and to transferring a portion of our riches to the most deprived, the welfare state has sometimes been said to be a compassionate state. In reality, it was inspired not so much by compassion or a respect for the poor or the unemployed as by the imperatives of the market economy, in other words, the desire, on the one hand, constantly to enlarge the networks of trade and consumerism, and the fear, on the other, that outside these networks recalcitrant ghettos would form that would pose a threat to order and good government. This would soon be made evident by the rapidity with which, once compassion seemed to have become less profitable or less necessary, one sought ways to control it or moderate it, always so as not to imperil the equilibrium and the competitiveness of the nation — that is, the economic well-being of the more prosperous classes.

The former state was also concerned with fair treatment for the less fortunate; it was during the Quiet Revolution that the first so-called social policies were conceived. But the compassion then was a *civic* compassion. It was dedicated to removing those obstacles that restricted an individual to his own private universe, kept him removed from the public domain, and prevented him from expressing himself and functioning as a citizen with all due rights. The democratization of the good life, closely linked, as it happens, to that of education, was not in and of itself the goal of social measures. They were a means of widening liberty, enlarging the shared community, just as economic prosperity was not the goal of politics, but one of the preconditions for its practice.

And so, with the triumph of the apolitical state, which is pure form and no content, a body with no other purpose than to reflect and serve the masses, a weightless *society* for a *community* that it constituted no more, that it had no more need or will to constitute, Tocqueville's prophecy was realized. Tocqueville, from the beginnings of the modern democratic state, foresaw as one of its possible consequences the paradoxical eradication of public concern through the establishment of a state dedicated entirely to the well-being of its population. "Private life in democratic times is so busy," he wrote at the end of *Democracy in America,* "so excited, so full of wishes and of work, that hardly any energy or leisure remains to each

individual for public life." At which point he imagined what
today we have before our very eyes:

> The first thing that strikes the observation is an
> innumerable multitude of men, all equal and alike,
> incessantly endeavouring to procure the petty and
> paltry pleasures with which they glut their lives. Each
> of them, living apart, is as a stranger to the fate of all
> the rest; his children and his private friends constitute
> for him the whole of mankind. As for the rest of his
> fellow citizens, he is close to them, but does not see
> them; he touches them, but does not feel them; he
> exists only in himself and for himself alone . . .
>
> Above this race of men stands an immense and
> tutelary power, which takes upon itself alone to
> secure their gratifications and to watch over their fate.
> That power is absolute, minute, regular, provident,
> and mild. It would be like the authority of a parent
> if, like that authority, its object was to prepare men
> for manhood; but it seeks, on the contrary, to keep
> them in perpetual childhood . . . For their happiness
> such a government willingly labours . . . it provides
> for their security, foresees and supplies their
> necessities, facilitates their pleasures, manages their
> principal concerns, directs their industry . . . .

It is true that Tocqueville, an aristocrat living in a dark
age, did not have the privilege of reading Lipovetsky or
Lyotard or any of the other bards of postmodern felicity. As
a result, what he saw was the vision of a despotic state. "Thus,"
he added, "it every day renders the exercise of the free agency
of man less useful and less frequent; it circumscribes the will
within a narrower range and gradually robs a man of all the

uses of himself." We ourselves know that this "despotism" is not the negation of individual liberty by an omnipresent and tentacular authority. It is, rather, the unconditional triumph of individual liberty and the obligation to be nothing but an individual, a private person, a taxpayer, a consumer, a watcher of television, and to act only in that capacity. As for the state, though it retains power — its power, in fact, continues to widen and increasingly to be a burden — it has lost any semblance of authority and the last scrap of high ground. It neither dominates the consciousness of individuals nor alienates them; it is the political arena itself that has been alienated, stripped of all purpose, become a pure means to ends that it accomplishes without having conceived them. It has been colonized, in short, and utterly domesticated.

All that survives in the aftermath are ancillary functions and forms: on the one hand, elected representatives who come and go, manage budgets, work tirelessly for reelection, and are strictly powerless politically; on the other, a bureaucratic apparatus that is powerful and secure, and must respond to ever more numerous and pressing demands that come from the public. And so, inevitably, it evolves into an enormous machine, all the heavier, all the more foreign and autocratic in that there is no longer anything transcendent to justify its existence and its actions. We no longer expect from this functional state or its leaders that they will propose or represent values, a history, a goal, only that they will be attentive to their market, that they will faithfully follow the fluctuations in public opinion (through polls), and that they will deliver the goods promptly and effectively — even when the goods to deliver are their own undoing, their own dissolution, in accordance with the need to "rethink" everything, to cut adrift all that remains from former times: solidarity with the weak and succour for those afflicted with material misfortune.

It is not surprising that politics, under such conditions, becomes (again) small and petty and ever less distinguishable from administration and publicity. Weighed down by the eternal in times past, now it has dissolved and vaporized, has been stripped of all substance and purpose by the wasting away of the very world where it had sought to establish itself. And so all parties, all political movements, whatever their stripe, even the most ideologically conservative, have no other choice today, if they want to be the least bit credible, but to take this decline into consideration and to show proof of their realism, in other words, to provide more of the same. For them to appeal to the populace for its support and its endorsement, they must strive to seduce the mass of individuals by appearing as like them as possible and proposing nothing they do not already know or desire. This explains the uniformity, the platitude, of today's political landscape: all camps, all groups, all opinion-makers speak the same language and defend, with minor differences, the same program, whose dependence on the slightest variations in the collective mood renders it fundamentally unstable, vulnerable to circumstance, nonexistent. We can understand why there is such harmony between the lowest common denominator of political thought and the lowest common denominator of television.

Another example of the tendency for political life to decline into insignificance could be found in Quebec, in the fate since about 1970 of the idea of independence, which was one of the last ideas with some coherence to have appeared on the public scene. Born along with Quebec's political consciousness itself, this secular idea that was the object of vast theoretical debates was able, towards the beginning of the sixties, to offer the nation a vision of itself living and acting in concert. It represented, in other words, the extension and full realization of the state of Quebec, in the republican sense

I outlined above: a way of being free, of assuming responsibility for one's society and perpetuating it, together. In this respect, independence did indeed constitute a *program*, a desire to make the real more human, to provide a horizon for public life. Moreover, it appeared distant, problematic, and difficult; it would require persuasion, reflection, an ongoing assessment of contingencies and the consequences resulting from action, an uneasiness and a breadth of vision, in short, all that was truly of a political order. It was not quite yet a modern — a lyric — idea.

This "lyricization" would be the great event of the seventies and the Parti Québécois, thanks to which, as we know, independence became a major electoral issue. But this success and this important increase in the clientele for independence was less the outgrowth of a genuine strategy than one of demographic circumstance: refusing to have anything to do with the old parties, (the parties of the old), those electors just newly received into the political community — electors of the lyric generation and the baby boom — allied themselves massively, as they do today, with the independence movement. The idea of independence, then, inevitably became their cause, and its fate was from then on intimately tied to their own.

The result was, in the first place, a more radical discourse, soon permeated by the other lyric ideologies of the time and a great surge of enthusiasm and militancy, which the leaders of the PQ had great difficulty containing or at least channelling, into viable political action. For the impatience of these new adults was then at its peak, as was their desire to seize power in order to rid themselves of the old world and to make it over into another that would conform to their aspirations. Independence for them appears an enormous festival, like those of their youth, where a united people, free of all constraints, sang the same song and stirred with the same joy: that of finding themselves together, alike, unique, and beautiful.

One is struck, when today one calls to mind the PQ conventions or the Saint-Jean Baptiste Day celebrations of the mid-seventies, by their similarity to the rock festivals or the student demonstrations of the preceding decade. It was the same climate, the same happiness born from the euphoria and the feeling of security associated with the simple fact of being together, merged into a crowd where all were as one, and all were the same. It was also the same feeling of power fed and amplified by the ideological decibels contained in rousing speeches and slogans, and the same domination, above all, by the rank and file — the same conviction that all legitimacy was born, resided, and had its end in numbers. For the democratic moral code, in the lyric mode, was simple: all that separates out becomes alienated and perverted; innocence and truth may be achieved only in a tightly knit group.

And so, the political idea of independence soon transformed itself into an emotion, a visceral need, a festive euphoria. Never has the nationalist flame burned so brightly as in those years of *le goût du Québec* — the taste of Quebec — of the ascendancy of *joual*, and of the veneration of a common culture that went by the name of *québécitude*.

But never, as well, has the cause of independence been so vulnerable. For in ceasing to be a call for the establishment of a common civic space and in becoming, rather, an invitation to remain oneself, to sustain and celebrate one's difference, it lost its prime motivating force. In this sense, its very success became a trap. All it would take would be for its young supporters to lose a bit of their ardour, to be distracted by other concerns, to simply age, or that some of their demands be symbolically met (Bill 101, agricultural zoning, the opening up of previously restricted hunting grounds), and the fever would drop, and with it, the political will for change. When all is said and done, the idea of independence suffered the same fate as any other political idea: wanting to seduce and reassure rather than make demands on its followers, wanting to be profitable and comfortable rather than distant and grave. Little by little it stripped itself of substance and today, it must be conceded, is little more than an empty slogan that works extremely well on television and whose "ratings" fluctuate from season to season, depending on circumstances and the whims of public opinion. The "founding of a territory," the taking possession of a "land," has been reduced to this querulous and petty notion of a "distinct society," which sees itself as nothing more than that, a society, and has nothing more to show for itself than its distinctiveness.

This is not the fault of the Parti Québécois, which did what it could. The devaluation of the idea of independence was only, in the last analysis, one of the consequences of the much wider phenomenon I have tried to describe in these pages, the final stage, perhaps, in that process of secularization that had been in the works for a long time: the overall desanctification of politics and the state. Desanctification did not simply deprive them both of their authority; it increasingly stripped them of all relevance. Insofar as it represented the last surviving embodiment of the sacred — however secularized and immersed in history — one might say that the state no longer exists; nor does politics as a domain dedicated to the expression and the consideration of the public will.

The postmodern individual has gone *beyond* politics. He has cut his ties with one more vestige of the past, with one more emblem of the world's burdensome weight. See him naked and free once more. See him happy and light.

THE ENZENSBERGER HYPOTHESIS

Like "the end of ideology," "the end of politics" is but another phrase signifying the triumph of the modern. Just as postmodernity is not the opposite of modernity, but the final stage in its evolution, so there is nothing paradoxical in seeing in the devaluation of the state, another sign of the lyric generation's influence and the full accomplishment of its mission. For to collaborate with modernity was not simply a matter of adhering to the most advanced theories and values of contemporary art and philosophy; it was also making oneself the instrument of that modern process dedicated to the desanctification of the world and the unburdening of existence.

That is why even the most hard-line lyric ideologies, and the most openly dissident, when we put them back in their overall context and see their subsequent effect on life and thought, appear to have been ideologies of consent rather than opposition, of obedience rather than of rebellion. Daniel Bell and Gerald Graff have ably analyzed this logic in relation to the literary and artistic avant-garde. When the capitalist economy, in order to continue to develop, no longer required as it had in the past a structured community with values and traditions that ensured order and stability, but rather a society that was extremely mobile, malleable, and open to continual change, and that was prepared constantly to reject what it had in favour of what was being offered it, any ideology advocating unending renewal and the abandonment of old models, any avant-garde fascinated with subversion and daring, ceased to be a threat to it and became its ally. The former enmity that opposed the poet or the revolutionary to the world of merchants and grocers gave way to a complicity grounded in the same need for "transgression," the same rejection of "limits," the same obliteration of the past, in other words, the same vision of an infinitely light world purged of constraints.

Certainly, lyric avant-gardists and ideologues continued to affect a healthy contempt for the barons of finance and others they saw as exploiters. This reflex, which they inherited from their predecessors, was another neoattitude. It was also a convenient way to remain blind to the collaboration that linked them objectively, as the Marxists would say, with the fate of the market economy and, in quieting their bad conscience, to leave themselves free to collaborate all the more actively. As for the reverse contempt, that of the merchant of former times who saw in the artist or in the innovator a troublemaker and a corrupter of youth, this continued to weaken, giving way to an acceptance and even an esteem that would have been a cause for celebration had it not derived quite so blatantly from self-interest. Advanced capitalism, as our modern economy has been termed by some, understood perfectly well how it could profit from the avant-gardist fervour and the constant calling into question of values, just as it profited directly from the domestication of the state and the trivialization of politics. What could suit it better than to be confronted with a society freed from all taboos, disabused of any preoccupations with the past, concerned solely with its own happiness, and, in accordance with Rimbaud's watchword, in constant pursuit of the new?

A generation of rupture and new beginnings, the lyric generation was thus in perfect harmony with the ultramodern society in which it lived. The examples of this affinity are legion. Here I will deal with two phenomena that, in addition to being representative of our times, are also particularly close to the spirit and the temperament of the lyric generation.

The first, of course, is mass communication, television in particular, a modern phenomenon whose evolution to all intents and purposes parallels that of the firstborn of the baby boom.

Strictly speaking, the birth and growth of the mass media largely preceded the appearance of this generation, since it dates at least from the thirties, when talking pictures made their debut and radio found its way into most households. We could go even farther back if we wanted to include book publishing for the masses and the popular press, whose heyday began in the nineteenth century. But the impact of those initial means of communication was paltry compared with that of television, because of factors such as their cumbersome technology, their slow evolution, the fact that their public was concentrated in cities and excluded vast swathes of the population, the small amount of leisure time available to the population, and finally their content, which was often didactic or elitist, and whose intent was to transmit to the people knowledge and values deriving from the educated classes. These factors limited their growth and prevented them from assuming a more prominent place in social and personal life. It was, if you like, the prehistory of the media age.

The age did not truly begin until television appeared on the scene just after the Second World War and became generally available during the fifties. The manner in which it arrived and the impact it had closely paralleled the lyric generation's own advance on the population. This, too, was a kind of invasion, as overwhelming as it was irresistible. Not only did television spread with the rapidity and the force of a tidal wave, but it was welcomed everywhere as the queen of the media, as the harbinger of a new age, as the perfect emblem and instrument for modernity. Its arrival caused immediate disquiet in the media landscape, obliging the other media to redefine themselves in its terms. For neither radio, nor newspapers, nor cinema were able to stand up to it. They had no other choice, if they wanted to survive, than to adapt, in other words, reinvent themselves as both the courtiers and the allies of television — bowing before it and trying as best they could to profit from its leavings. They became, in short, its parasites.

In Quebec (and the rest of Canada) we can divide the history of television into two distinct phases. The first was brief, from about 1952 to 1960, when production and broadcast were still a state monopoly. It was the phase that we might characterize as idealistic. Coming as they did from radio, the written press, theatre, or literature, where they had already developed a certain approach to mass communication, the producers of this heroic period conceived of television as a means of education and information whose primary role, it seemed to them, was to bestow culture and enlightenment on the people. While escape and entertainment also figured among their concerns, their priorities were television drama and symphony concerts, public affairs programs and educational shows for children. Television viewers today would find such awkwardness touching and naïve.

The change occurred when the state, in response to a growing demand that the public network could not satisfy, decided to "liberalize" the airwaves and opened them up to

competition from private producers. This was the beginning
of a new phase, in the course of which television, while
continuing to enlarge its empire, would redefine itself entirely
and bit by bit assume the appearance it has today. The
networks multiplied, broadcast hours lengthened, colour
made its appearance, then the satellite, cable, specialized
programming, the VCR, and so on until television, already
mistress without peer in the media, became siren to our souls
and to our lives, ruling our hours, lulling us gently with
picture and sound, all the while swallowing us whole.

What is certain is that this phenomenal development
could not have taken place without the active, unfailing
collaboration of the lyric generation and the entire baby
boom, who have always enjoyed a privileged relationship with
television. It was thanks to their enormous numbers and
homogeneity, their leisure time and inextinguishable thirst
for well-being and stimulation without end, that television
was able to grow as it did and to become much more than a
gigantic industry: it became the nerve centre for an entire
symbolic circulatory system animating modern society. The
empire of television was thus only one of the provinces of an
infinitely vaster empire where the lyric generation held sway
over the world. But television was a province particularly dear
to the lyric generation's heart, which it indulged unstintingly,
for of all the provinces that depended on its empire this was
the most loyal, the most loving, and the one that reflected it
most faithfully and most happily.

But the lyric generation brought more to television than
a sympathetic and enthusiastic public. There was also this
generation's visceral need never to lose touch with its own
kind, to feel united always, to be swept along together, to
respond in unison, and to inhabit and possess one body, one
enormous soul. And that is exactly what television offered:

not so much ideas or emotions, but the sense of togetherness, the day-to-day experience of the global village, the euphoric sense of sharing and of communication. Furthermore, television answered this need in the most benign way imaginable, for it required no commitment, no actual encounter with others. Even as they reach out to me and allow me to lose myself in them, these words and faces cannot touch me; I can turn the set off whenever I choose.

But there is more. As Hans-Magnus Enzensberger puts it in *Mediocrity and Delusion,* what set television apart and the reason it was superior to other media was that it was much more successful than radio or the written word, for example, in drawing near (without quite realizing it at first, but that was only a question of time) to the utter absence of content that is the ideal of all mass communication. Only television was able to imbue its public with *pure* communication, to monopolize thought and feeling while sparing it any message or program whatsoever, any need to decode what was being transmitted. Nor was anything imposed on the public other than a besotted fascination it was free to prolong or cut short as it wished. In that respect, adds Enzensberger, the television viewer comes as close as an adult can come to the bliss of infancy, when the organism is raw receptivity alone, a passive and euphoric assimilation of all stimuli, opening onto a sensuous universe of sounds, colour, and indistinct and ever-changing forms whose meaning it has no need to define or discover, and even less to register and make allowances for.

The resemblance between the mental state of Enzensberger's television viewer and the psychology of the lyric generation as I've tried to portray it is clear. In both, the world is but a kind of phantasm with no substance of its own, with no ultimate purpose, constrained by no a priori meaning. Instead, it is entirely open, totally at the mercy of desire and will, identical again to the flux of audiovisual signals in whose guise reality appears to the newborn: impermanent, intimately linked to its actions and perceptions, and therefore at any moment alterable or dispensable. "Buzzing, blooming confusion," said William James. And so this unreal reality, this minimally ontological presence, requires no interpretation by those who cross its path, no study, no apprenticeship, only the capacity to feel, see, hear, and experience pleasure — a pleasure that is all the greater in that it does not know if it issues from the world outside, or if it is the music of its very own being, or both at once.

And so we can understand the complicity that was established from the beginning between the lyric generation and the world of television, and that has been reinforced ever since. If the new adult saw himself reflected in television to that extent and to such an extent made it his companion in his social and private life, it is because it enabled him every day, in a very real way, to sustain and confirm his modern, distinctive "view of the world." Seated in front of his small screen, he could relive over and over the event — or non-event — that defined him: his youth preserved, confrontation and capitulation sidestepped once again, the world at his feet like a kingdom he has only to seize without risk or danger and that he is free to transform or to do away with any time he wants. Television was the closest possible analogue to the lyric view of the world as lightness, as pure and infinite "zappability."

But this complicity was possible only if television, on its side, went along with it. And not only did it do so, but its complicity became its new vocation, the secret of its success. We might say, in fact, that the second phase in its history — which is where we still find ourselves today — consisted in television's developing a better and better understanding of what its public demanded, in devising increasingly effective strategies to respond to this demand, and in constantly renewing itself so as to draw ever closer to the end point defined by the Enzensberger hypothesis. In other words, the clientele drawn from the lyric generation gave television the opportunity to break totally with earlier models that had prevented it from realizing its potential, and enabled it to give full rein to its natural inclinations, to finally and absolutely become itself.

Since the sixties, there has been a growing decrease in the amount of informational and educational material, and a clear priority accorded to *reflecting* the audience and *entertaining* it, resulting in the dwindling, if not the complete disappearance, of content and message in favour of stimulation and well-being.

The golden rule of television today is not to speak to the audience, to pass on to it some piece of information, to show it one thing or another, but simply to grab on to it and not let go, to stay close always to its familiar universe and to its most obvious expectations, without ever disturbing or disorienting it in any way. To this end, television is aiming ever lower, becoming increasingly facile and avoiding like the plague anything that would risk tiring the spectator or requiring any response other than abandonment or complacent agreement. It is a question of bringing the entire universe into each household and into the life of every spectator; to bring it in, to shrink it, to accommodate it, and in doing so strip the universe of any foreignness, of any true otherness, in order to put it *within the reach* of every individual, on a level with his own small life and large opinions.

Television, in this sense, is not only hostile to content, but essentially narcissistic. Its goal is to seduce and reassure viewers, repeating over and over that they are right to be who they are, to think what they think, and to ignore what they ignore. The "window on the world" is in reality a magic mirror in which viewers, through images of the world, endlessly contemplate their own image and own life, and find them infinitely just and good. Their little screen makes them feel that they can be everywhere, see everything, know everything, delight in everything, in short, hold sway over the world without the slightest confrontation or the slightest struggle being required.

And directors and hosts excel in treating viewers like the kings they want to be, and that they indeed become from the moment they turn on their sets. Comfortably installed in an armchair and wielding their zapper like a sceptre, they select their universe, or kingdom, for the evening and pass judgements, proclaim laws, admire or are moved, and delight in the measure of their power until late into the night . Everything must humbly defer to the sovereign's pleasure, to the acknowledgement of his rule, to the sway of his law, or risk banishment from the airwaves or a shameful exile to a time slot with low ratings.

Officially, of course, television continues to pass for, and to take itself for, an instrument of popular education. Its programming draws liberally on the tradition of "high" culture — operas, novels, cinema classics, history, the natural sciences, and so on. It finds there a rich lode of material to sustain its "creative" bulimia, and to enable it to diversify the options it offers the public, all the while giving it a clear conscience. But the appearance of literature, film, music, or even philosophy on television does not simply expand or democratize their traditional audience. It is also a form of dispossession. Forsaking a universe that is their own, where the purpose, the meaning and the value of a work is contingent on other works occupying the same universe, these cultural artifacts enter a totally different world, where the rules and logic bear no resemblance to those they were familiar with in the past, for these now are the rules and logic of television. In short, the context has changed completely, and with it the very meaning of those works that have been sent into exile beyond the confines of the territory where they were born.

This misdirection shows itself in many ways. For example, the choices made by directors and programmers from among the pool of literary and musical "products" at their disposal will not primarily be based on musical or literary criteria, but rather on the televisual potential of the works and the ease with which they can be transformed into audiovisual entertainments that are as seductive and as innocuous as possible. And so the works selected will always be the most facile: Conan Doyle rather than Virginia Woolf, Puccini or Tchaikovsky rather than Berg or Bach. And even if by chance television chooses to accommodate more demanding works and thought for the betterment of the people, it will adapt them and make them "telegenic," in other words, as attractive and agreeable to viewers as the other distractions being broadcast at the same time on competing channels. Mozart will be rendered as lively as the latest pop star; Plato's opinions will be confronted by those of a fashionable young essayist; *The Man Without Qualities* will be relieved of its *longueurs,* put into dialogue, and converted into a series of twelve elaborately produced episodes shot on location in eight languages, with a surprise happy ending. And that is the way — softened, lightened, recycled, and stripped of any power to disturb — that high culture will reach the viewers, according them just what all the images in their cathodic mirror routinely provide: escape, relaxation, an unstinting confirmation of their excellence and royal standing.

Whether it be politics, arts and letters, religion, or commerce, anything that wants to address the populace today has no other choice, if it wants to be heard, but to avail itself of this avenue, or if it cannot, at least to adopt its logic and methods. It must in turn become a mirror and a diversion, simplifying and minimizing its content, maximizing its image, as much as it can. To no one's surprise, that is where advertising has succeeded admirably, with its shorter and shorter spots burdened less and less with text, followed closely by rock with the invention of the "videoclip," the ultimate in televisual communication, where the ideal described by Enzensberger seems finally to have been achieved. And so one may easily predict — and we already see the signs everywhere around us — that the influence of television will not only grow, but that this growth will result in a runaway "videoclipization" not only of television itself, but of all other forms of public discourse, which will become increasingly indistinguishable from media discourse, the norm and model for modern communication.

Outside television — but is there anything, still, *outside* television? — the phenomenon takes the form of what I call the rule of adaptability, the requirement that any idea, any argument, be strongly "televisable," not only in lending itself to simplification, but in having enough "punch," so that, once its content has been rendered banal, if not done away with completely, there will still remain an image, a word, a figure, a gunshot, or some stimulus that will have enough impact to stop the viewer's hand as it reaches for the remote control. Pop stars, some political figures, Pope John Paul II, terrorists of all sorts, as well as a few writers and intellectuals, are past masters at the art of being unfailingly "clipable."

Even when it does not influence them directly and does not afford them the blessing of its own airwaves, television thus tends to control all means of expression through the

pressure it applies and the need it creates for them to take it
into account and to try as best they can to compete, which
means trying to resemble videoclipization in one way or
another. We see this in journalism, in film and theatre, even
in literature, where minimal content and the aesthetics of
sensation make great advances day by day. This phenomenon
has made itself felt in teaching, where the modernization of
pedagogic practices consists, for the most part, in simplifying
subject matter, increasing options (intellectual zapping), and
hewing as close as possible to a world familiar to the children,
thus guaranteeing that there be less and less difference for the
pupil between his half days at school and the rest of his day
spent in front of the television set.

All that is commonplace today, and so it is a waste of effort
to denounce the pomp and dominance of television. But this
does not absolve us from understanding the medium and in
the process coming to a better understanding of what characterizes our time. In this respect, the point I most want to make
is that the relationship between contemporary "telephilia" —
that is, the exponential increase in audiences, viewing hours,
the number of broadcasters, and both the quantity and quality
of equipment — and the no less striking rise in the level of
insignificance (in the most exact sense of the word) and of
stupidity (in a sense no less exact) which typifies both
television's production and its ever widening sphere of influence, is neither accidental nor contradictory. All indications,
as the Enzensberger hypothesis predicted, are that on the
contrary the more television expands its empire, the more
meaning, and the *need* for meaning, diminishes. To put it
another way: the more present television becomes, the more
absent the world is. What the cause is and what the effect is
are impossible to say. We find ourselves confronted with one
of those "epistemological loops" dear to Edgar Morin. A is

the cause of B, which is the cause of A, which is the cause of B, and where it all leads, no one knows.

Now, turning also in this loop is the lyric generation, which saw itself reflected in the televised image so completely, because it responded to something deep within itself and expressed most vividly some of its deepest desires. And so, is that state of inferiority to which television is in the process of reducing all other forms of communication a simple accident of history to be explained only with reference to technological development? Or may we see in it another sign — another consequence — of the "lyricization" of the world, now in the firm control, body and soul, of its new masters?

THE CONSUMPTION
OF THE WORLD

The connection between the rapid growth of television and the economy of consumption, another syndrome dear to our modernity and therefore particularly revealing, could not be more direct, as is clearly demonstrated by what Jacques Godbout refers to as the interminable "mercantile murmuring" of television today. If these two phenomena are that closely linked, if they suit one another so well, it is because there is an even stronger affinity between them than one might think at first glance. Both have their roots in the same metaphysical stance, in the same way of living in the world and dealing with it. Indeed, both have been assumed by the lyric generation with the same consistency and enthusiasm, as if this generation derived from the one as from the other the most effective means to accomplish its destiny and to make its presence felt in the world.

Already, in purely quantitative terms, the contemporary explosion in consumer activity, like telephilia, can be attributed almost completely to a sudden increase in the buying public. This, in turn, may be traced to the lyric generation, which is not only great in numbers, but acquired in adolescence, if not in childhood, the habit of immoderate consumption, even though its means were then more limited. Arrived at adulthood, the generation could at last give free rein to its enthusiasm, and at the same time impose its logic on the rest of society. The fact is that the lyric generation made an ideal clientele. It had good jobs, which provided both money and the leisure to spend it, and its psychology was tailor-made to bolster and constantly recharge the consumer marketplace. Its expectations and needs were considerable; it teemed with desires, which it had become accustomed to satisfying without delay. And its passion for progress, rupture, and discovery made it eminently receptive to anything novel. And finally, it was a gregarious generation that reacted *en masse,* in vast collective surges, wanting nothing so much as to share similar tastes and experiences, which made it vulnerable to what was fashionable and to trends of all description. All of this, of course, was no surprise to advertisers and merchants, who knew exactly how to appeal to this multitudinous Narcissus and how to gain its favour.

And so began what has been called the age of mass consumption. But this expression is deceptive, because consumption has always been a mass phenomenon, insofar as it consists in procuring the necessities of life — food, lodging, and clothing. What changed, rather, was the consumption of goods and services once considered frills or luxuries, and available only to a tiny fraction of the population. Travel, leisure activities, shows, books, gadgets of all sorts, therapy, and courses in personal development were the sectors where the "massification" of demand was remarkable, as it was in those sectors that furnished luxury items providing both pleasure and prestige: delicacies and fine foods, interior decoration, new religions, designer clothes, and so on. These objects and services, however superfluous they may have seemed objectively, were henceforth considered musts, items without which life was no longer worth living. What in their parents' day would have appeared a sumptuous standard of living became for the children of the lyric generation a normal way of life to which they were entitled. It was as simple as that.

But the rise of consumption in the modern world was not only a question of figures and sales and the frantic escalation of supply and demand. It was reflected also, more importantly, by a no less significant growth in the value accorded the activity of consumption and the position it occupied in the lives of individuals as in the life of society. For some time, consumption had been showing signs of increased autonomy, to employ a fashionable term, detaching itself from its traditional function, which was to facilitate the realization of other goals (supporting life and maintaining production power). Now it required no justification or purpose beyond itself: to consume for the joy of consuming, for the constant pleasure, the feverish cycle of desire and satisfaction it was able to sustain. Today, autonomy itself does not suffice. Having become the goal for all other activity and the standard against which it is measured, consumption has achieved a kind of economic — and moral — *sovereignty* over our lives and our society.

There is something ironic in this development. We are familiar with the vicious circle in which classic capitalism, or capitalism in its raw state, trapped the workers: everything they earned went towards their expenses, so that they could work more. In the process, the bourgeoisie became rich. Little by little, however, and especially in the prosperous years that followed the Second World War, capitalism mellowed. It allowed for a certain liberation of the worker, his becoming bourgeois, because it consisted primarily in the freeing up of an increasing proportion of his income, which he could henceforth direct towards other goals, bourgeois goals such as the purchase of property, investment, savings, the putting together of an inheritance, and above all, the education of children, all of which, unlike consumption, had a stake in time, in transforming daily work into something that would endure.

Late capitalism, both in its neoliberal and social-democratic variants, has brought us back to total consumption. Not only is the entire production of work instantly transformed into merchandise designed to be used on the spot, but this consumption has become, once more, the primary, if not the only, justification for work. We might even say that it precedes it, in time as well as in principle: we acquire before we pay, then we work to pay for what has been acquired and what, once paid for, will already be useless or used up. That is the logic behind what is called consumer credit. Even before it has been earned, nothing remains of one's revenue that can be applied to goals other than those already achieved.

This regression seems all the more paradoxical in that it occurred at a time when workers have never been less downtrodden; in other words, never have they had as much disposable income once the necessities of their daily life had been assured. Never, in short, have we been as rich or as free not to dedicate all our holdings to consumption. And yet we spend everything we earn, and even more, to buy goods and services that not only do not endure, but are designed to deteriorate. It is as though we know how to do nothing but consume, as if we cannot conceive of any other use for what our work produces but squandering it instantly on gadgets, on fleeting pleasures, on whatever is the latest rage.

And so, because the whole economy is at stake, there is no other choice but to keep consumption alive and forever growing, to provide goods and services that are always new and always ephemeral, always more advanced than those of the preceding generation, and always more susceptible to being surpassed by the next in line. It is what experts call planned obsolescence. Exemplified not long ago by the automobile and clothing industries, this syndrome is now rife in the area of new technologies: electronic, computer, or telecommunications. Their products must be constantly evolving, and the user is enjoined to be on the cutting edge of progress, ever prepared to divest himself of what he owns and to improve his system thanks to the new toy that has been placed in his path.

But what one often forgets is that this law of systematic antiquation is not something accidental or new. On the contrary, it is in the very nature of consumption to devour things, burn them up, reduce them to nothing through use and wear, and so condemn them always to be discarded and replaced by others. Food, the most basic consumption, a candidate for obsolescence if ever there was one, provides the best example. As the word implies, consumption is to do away with, to consume.

What is new today, what is modern, is the scope of this consumption, the fact that everything or practically everything is grist for the mill, including goods once considered durable, that is, immune from the reductive process. Lodging comes readily to mind, household appliances, even knowledge and culture. Any object, any idea, any *person* is there to be acquired and then rejected as soon as something better or newer — a more modern idea, a more attractive individual — comes along to replace it and plunge it into obsolescence.

And so the end of ideology is perhaps, in the last analysis, only one consequence of a general law decreeing that nothing endures that has already been employed once, that has been stripped of its original value through ownership and use. For the consumer, everything is disposable and can be discarded once he has done with it. He is not a slave to his possessions, he does not worship them; what he venerates, what is priceless in his eyes, is their novelty and his pleasure in discovering them. The consumer is essentially a creature of love at first sight. Once the novelty has evaporated, he throws away objects, which become just things, and he throws away ideologies, now just lifeless arguments with outdated words and ideas. In the marketplace of intellectual consumption, thoughts, theories, paradigms, and other explicative models behave more or less as do cars, furniture, or clothing; they prevail for as long as it takes for them to be passed around, and then they are relegated to the dump to rust away.

The increase in what is consumable is therefore not only an economic issue. It is also, above all perhaps, the sign or consequence of a major moral and philosophical shift, a direct product of the modern revolution; in the absence of established traditions grounded in contemplation and respect, forms of apprenticeship, and the surrendering of the self, consumption and consumerism become the only natural way to treat the world and to relate to it. When an individual feels that he has been invested with the mission and the right to break with everything and to begin anew, when he swears only by his desires and nothing in his path has any weight, how can he care about permanence in the world? How can he help but see the world as an immense market where he can explore, acquire, and *use* everything, only to toss it away when the spirit moves him?

The relationship with consumer products thus provides the same sort of euphoria as television, a delight akin to the bliss of the newborn to whom the universe has not yet offered any constraint or resistance. Like television, consumption does away both with reality and *semantics*. Consumption strips the object of its otherness, deprives it of that foreignness and solidity that were its own — and that conferred upon it its existence in the world — and reduces it to the status of something empty and available, just as television dissolves objects into a blissful spectacle of sound and light. With both consumerism and television, the individual finds himself faced with nothing that will deny him his desire of the moment, that will require the least compromise, deference, or suffering, not even the suffering that comes with compassion. The universe has become perfectly light; it is there, as simple as that, silent and accessible. It has become a *plastic* universe, as Roland Barthes said, whose malleability is total.

This fever of consumption provides us with another illustration of the Enzensbergerian hypothesis of "zero content." A hypothesis that could be extrapolated to a more general theory that would account for the behaviour and attitudes of the lyric generation: the theory of *the world at degree zero.*

Since the beginning of this book, I have made frequent use of the word "world," in which I hope my readers will have recognized the influence of Hannah Arendt. This word, for her, represents "the human household built upon the earth," that is to say, the true, the only authentically human, environment for the human condition. Distinct from nature, which is the context for life, and from eternity, which is the locus for timeless essences, the world is the unique homeland for man, constructed with his own hands, out of his own freedom, to escape the eternity that overwhelms him and the instability of the vital processes that enslave and kill him. To be in the world is to belong to time and not to eternity, and to establish beyond the ken of nature's time, which is an interminable cycle of endings and beginnings, a time of man, which houses him, all the while being his creation, and inscribes his fleeting existence in a *continuum* that is both fragile and immortal.

The world, thus understood, is not first and foremost what dominates or transcends us. On the contrary, it depends entirely on ourselves, on the need we have of it and on the presence we accord it. It endures only insofar as our lives and thoughts, brief and perishable as they are, render it imperishable. Made of words, thoughts, and objects not given us by nature or the gods, but created by men to enlighten and preserve their humanity, it is what every individual receives when he first comes among his peers; it is what he safeguards and enlarges through his own actions before passing them on in turn to those that follow. And so, the world is both a gift and a work, accorded to and enhanced by every person. It is what shelters, what frames the acts of each, and at the same time makes them possible. It is what limits and frees. It is what makes us human.

For Hannah Arendt, housing could not be more different from consumption. The latter for her is but another aspect of work, that is, the utilization and destruction of nature in the sole interest of keeping intact those functions needed to sustain life. If consumption is a necessary foundation for action and work, it does not suffice for building a world and passing it on. On the contrary, it is in freeing ourselves from the vital processes and logic of consuming, which rules the acts and thoughts of "animal laborans," that we may escape the controlling influence of our own mortality in our day-to-day life and assert our sense of belonging to the world.

That is why there is nothing more terrible to the author of *The Human Condition* than what we call the society of consumption, where the only meaning we accord our acts is to work towards biological ends, which are the satisfaction of our immediate needs, the expression of our vitality, and the acquisition and enhancement of our comfort and our happiness. The consuming life, seen in this light, can derive only from a *refusal of the world*, which is a form of desertion. And what concept of the world, of the permanence and fragility of the world, could the consumer, and his Siamese twin, the viewer of television, possibly have? Everything that exists, in their view, is made to nourish and amuse them, to be desired and devoured on the spot. One could say of them what Alain Finkielkraut said of the postmodern individual: "It is as a *tourist* that he views the world and strolls through the great department store of humanity." As a tourist, that is, with greed and ennui, like someone for whom his homeland has become an immense attraction, a reservoir of amusing objects, all cheap and disposable.

To be delivered into the hands of this consumption is therefore the worst thing that could happen to Arendt's world. It is as though, all at once, the world lost its sense of purpose and no longer had any weight, reality, or durability, as though it was borne up no more by the allegiance and actions of men, and nothing was left between it and its own precariousness. Where the common household had once stood, the jungle has ·reasserted all its rights — an appropriate image for the world's ruin and abandonment.

Are today's consumer and televiewer nostalgic for a lost world? One would sometimes think so, given the increased interest in ecology, which is like an expression of remorse or disgust at having consumed so much.

But ecological thought is ambiguous. At its most lucid — which is often when it is most cynical or pessimistic — one might say that it does indeed conceive of the world in Arendt's terms and sees in the devastation of nature the devastation of the world itself, that is to say, the feeling men have for their connection with what surrounds them. This way of thinking is not inspired by conservationism or the fear of no longer being able to consume. It is inspired, on the contrary, by an attachment to nature, to its beauty, and to what I would call its humanity, because this beauty and humanity have been betrayed, have been robbed of their strength for want of that world that both resided in and guaranteed nature its future. Thus understood, the ecological consciousness is one of loss. It can only, therefore, be a tragic consciousness.

But it must not be confused with the other version of the ecology movement, the Edenic version, if you like, which in recent years has become one of the favourite forms of expression for the lyric ideology, and therefore one of the major leitmotifs of media murmurings. This noisily militant ecological triumphalism, if it had any notion of the world, or culture, would see that they are not allies but the sworn enemies of nature, which has been baptized, in any case, with new, more modern names to avoid any humanistic or anthropomorphic bias: "the environment," "the planet," "the biosphere," and so on. For nature here is only material, a stock of resources that must be "managed" and "conserved," not for its beauty or intrinsic value, but out of fear for its eventual exhaustion and the impact such an exhaustion would have on the life and happiness of individuals.

And so there is nothing surprising in the fact that industry and big business, after briefly feeling threatened by moral conservationists, soon came to use their slogans as instruments of their own growth. There is a deep affinity between consumerism and an ecology movement based on a denunciation of the world and its human works. They are two sides of the same coin, not enemies. Both draw on the same logic, the same view of a nature that, while no longer appearing infinitely renewable, remains nonetheless available, consisting of things to use and devour for the benefit of the economy and the pleasure of consumers. One can see this lyric ecology as a kind of reflex by virtue of which the sated consumer, fearing suddenly to run out of food, chooses to moderate or to defer the satisfaction of desires so as not to risk being totally deprived. It is, therefore, a form of behaviour that is still, quintessentially, concerned with sustaining life and promoting well-being.

But the world, those surroundings born of human artifice, is not something that can be depolluted, like the air of our cities or the water of our rivers; to clean it up would mean, on the contrary, to destroy it. Nor is the world something that can be conserved, like tropical forests or "green" spaces. The only possible haven for it is as the dwelling place of our memories, admiration, and works.

THE YOUNG LIFE

Humanity is younger and younger.

Milan Kundera
The Art of the Novel

And what about existence? What happens to existence when the world becomes weightless and what Lipovetsky has called the age of emptiness finally takes hold? What can it then mean to exist? What then orders and animates life?

What occurs is what happened to the lyric generation once it attained adulthood: a giddiness, a euphoria, a feeling of deliverance, purity, and innocence so absolute that it seemed that life and the universe were beginning anew, that paradise was once more at hand, and that, over and above everything that had distorted it, that had kept it buried so long beneath the world's leaden weight, that first authentic plenteousness of being alive was once more seeing the light of day.

Nothing better evokes this mood than the last pages of Milan Kundera's *The Book of Laughter and Forgetting*, when Edwige and her friends, assembled on an offshore island, outside the world as it were, have the impression, once divested of their clothes, that they have returned to the age of Daphnis. "On the other side of the inhuman world our civilization imprisons us in," "back to the times before Christianity crippled mankind," there where "burdensome traditions" no longer hold sway, on this *vacation,* in this absence of the (old) world, resides true happiness, total freedom, the pure lightness of being, in other words, the crowning existential apotheosis of modern liberation.

What the dissolution of the world brought with it, then, was the joy of escaping from age and time. That is because the world, and concern for the perpetuation and precariousness of the world, is the hallmark of aging, as well as its prerogative. If an adult is someone who has renounced the self and stepped aside, it is because he has become conscious of his responsibility where the world is concerned, and that this consciousness, in addition to weighing him down, has inevitably set limits on what up till then was regarded as his freedom. But in a world at degree zero, the adult and the old have no place. Their consciousness and gravity would be an embarrassment, would lower their status and doom them to see themselves and be seen by others as foreign. That is why Edwige and her friends, who are perhaps all about forty, can feel such a kinship with Daphnis and Chloé, who are forever fifteen or sixteen and will never become adults. Like Adam and Eve before the Fall, that is to say, before they "fell" into the world, they enjoy eternal youth.

And such, it seems to me, is the privilege that has been accorded those I have called the *new* adults of the lyric generation. Unlike the adults who came before, and who were forever distanced from their youth by their responsibility for the world, they provide the singular spectacle of adults who have not aged, adults who have been spared the burden of adult consciousness. They may soon reach the half-century mark, but their desires, their souls, and sometimes even their bodies will have conserved the ardour and beauty of adolescence. For they have not had to yield or compromise themselves. At an age when men and women, not that long ago, were considered (and considered themselves) old, they have continued to live as they did when they were young — casual, unfettered, all spontaneity and ardent desire, wholeheartedly dedicated to change, to progress, and to the perpetual discovery of what is new and better — to an existence, in short, as infinitely light and carefree as when they were twenty.

I have already provided several illustrations of the young life, which is to the lyric generation what the "good life" was to the ancient Greeks, beginning with television and consumption as examples of an essentially infantile relationship with the world. I could give many others; sociological studies and society columns are full of them. The behaviour patterns acquired in childhood and adolescence — congregating always with others of the same age, experiencing and doing the same things at the same time, feeling oneself surrounded, swept along, reassured by a generational wave — have been maintained and even reinforced later in life. But the most obvious examples, of course, concern the amorous behaviour of these new adults. All their strategies for reinventing love each day — their sexual freedom; their undying faith in love at first sight; their skill in cruising and performing the romantic slalom; their reluctance to commit themselves, as they put it, because passion must have its due, their marital fidelity even, subject always to renegotiation; and finally their predilection for indulging in an obsessive analysis and exposure of their life experience and feelings, tirelessly sifted, put on display, and weighed in the balance — give them the aura of perpetual adolescents, as fascinated now as they were at puberty with the limitless torments of the heart and the senses. And the same is true for physical conditioning, athletic pursuits, clothing, bearing, literary or musical tastes, the return to school beyond the age of forty, or even, where intellectual activities are concerned, the obsession with the cutting edge of the avant-garde at any price. It all comes down to the fact that people today in their forties or fifties, set next to those of years gone by, would seem, in body as well as in spirit, incomparably lighter, less conventional and far less behind the times. If one could see them alongside adults of their age from times past, they would more closely resemble their sons and daughters.

We have seen how this generation, unlike all others before it, was not obliged to renounce youth in order to gain access to society and make a place for itself. It got the very biggest and best place immediately. Never having had to learn the world, to settle down and temper its expectations, it could not think of itself in any other way but young, desiring, destined always to move ahead with all options open. And it refused the very idea of letting go. To grow old was inconceivable. To grow old was tantamount to surrender.

This perpetuation of the miracle of eternal youth was not entirely due to the weakness of the generations that preceded the lyric generation. It was due, as well, to another, equally crucial factor: the weakness of the generation that came *afterwards*.

Youth, in point of fact, is a relative attribute. If our parents have aged, it is because we were there behind them to occupy the territory or stage in life that they had left untended. But when there is no one to follow, when the young, as they become older, no longer have to step aside, when they are no longer displaced or dislodged by the younger behind them, why should they become old? Why should they not continue, even as the wrinkles deepen on their faces, to consider themselves as the natural custodians of youth?

In more prosaic terms, when the average age of the population increases, the ceiling of youth, or the proportion of those who belong to groups younger in years, rises along with it. Which is why the aging of the population, which is so troubling to demographers and politicians, also implies a rejuvenation. That, in any case, is what the example of the lyric generation teaches us: it is not because fewer children are being born; it is not because the proportion of those under twenty is shrinking; it is not, in short, because the age pyramid is becoming a diamond that the spirit of youth — its ardour, daring, and impenitent lyricism — is about to vanish from our societies. On the contrary, this ethos is spreading, expanding, becoming eternal. What is new is that the young of today are forty to fifty years old. Despite their age they are still young and still imbued with all the goodly virtues of youth.

There are, of course, important distinctions to be made between the two factors that have enabled the lyric generation to remain young. If the first, the weakness of its predecessors, can be ascribed to circumstances beyond the lyric generation's control and from which it was simply content to profit, the second, the weakness of its successors, was entirely and uniquely its own creation, our work as adults. It is we who, freed from our elders by the grace of history, have arranged things in such a way as to remain free, too, in respect to those who came or who might have come in our wake. Having seen our parents cede their place before us, we have chosen not to step aside in favour of those who followed.

Not to step aside is not to become *parents* in our turn. For to do so would have been to accept the unacceptable: to betray ourselves, join the enemy camp, grow old. The parent is always old, because the world is no longer open to him as a field for conquest or for desire. The world, now, is a territory to be inhabited by his children and himself, and whose fate is in his hands. He must no longer struggle against the world, but must, on the contrary defend it, stabilize it, and assure its permanence on behalf of those for whom he is responsible. And so he has the paradoxical role of opposing the young while at the same time embracing them, delimiting their territory while at the same time surrendering it to them. The parent is also old because he is by definition one who passes on, or who consents to do so — who *is* the past. In making a legacy of his life, he places it in the hands of those who come after, bids farewell to himself in advance and to his power and desires. He leaves his youth behind for good and all.

To reject the parental condition is thus just one more way for the lyric generation to remain true to itself. Delivered from the weight of the world, how could the new adult want or be able to assume it and pass it on? How could one who defined himself entirely in terms of rupture accept being an instrument of continuity, and in so doing, to vanish from the scene? And so, a reciprocal relationship was created between eternal youth and the refusal of parentage, whereby the one implied the other, and the first was both the precondition for and the consequence of the second. Because I do not want to surrender my youth, I cannot see myself as a parent, and because I am not a parent, I can preserve my youth.

The first consequence of this refusal, of course, was a lack of children. The drop in the birth rate, according to demographers, who even speak in terms of the "sterility" typical of this generation, may be explained by a wide variety of factors, including biological "megafactors" relating to the equilibrium of the population. One can imagine what would have happened if all the women of the lyric generation and the baby boom would have had as many children as their mothers or even one or two fewer, if, in other words, the disturbance in the birth rate had been prolonged through yet another generation, had been amplified and multiplied exponentially. Surely a return to normal was in the cards. It need not have taken place as rapidly or as drastically, nor resulted in another disturbance, this one the mirror image of its predecessor. But in the wake of the baby boom a decrease in the birth rate was both natural and predictable.

Besides this balancing effect, a number of cultural factors may also explain the infertility of the lyric generation: the extension of studies, the weakening of religion, a modification in work habits and lifestyles, and so on. The economic context must also have played a role, although it is difficult to assess with any exactitude; after all, unlike the thirties, the drop this time in the number of births coincided with an unprece-dented period of economic prosperity and security. The gen-eralized use of contraceptives, often considered one of the causes of the phenomenon, could have been only a catalytic or facilitating factor: it is not because women take the pill that they have no more children; it is because they want no more children that they take the pill.

A decisive element, therefore, was a change in women's attitudes to maternity. But this phenomenon was itself rooted in an even more fundamental change that involved the defi-nition of sexual roles and identity not only within the couple and society as a whole, but in the consciousness and the lives of individuals themselves. When adults, men as well as women, cease to consider maturity as a time to give up their own expectations and devote themselves to those of the younger generation, when the end of youth is regarded as an irreparable loss or a betrayal of the self, then marriage, family, and all other behaviour linked to procreation are inevitably devalued. The first sign of an adult's freedom to remain young, the very condition of this freedom, will always be not to have any children.

Whatever the *causes* of the lower birth rate, causes so numerous, so difficult to disentangle and so recalcitrant that they render any indictment and any regret both inappropriate and useless, the principal *effect* could not be clearer: its infertility, or at least its drastically reduced fecundity, spared the lyric generation that lowering of status ordinarily reserved for adults when youth arrives on the scene, that is, when parents see their own offspring rising up behind them. Once more, there is no question here of a plot fomented in advance by the new adults to protect their position. On the contrary, it was quite spontaneously, and with the conviction that they were doing what was best, that they became the first generation of nonparents. "What was best" meant what was best for their own happiness and therefore for the happiness of all, their own liberation being in their view the liberation of the entire human condition, which had been enslaved and ground down for millennia by the burden of reproduction.

But however noble their intentions, everything unfolded as though the adults of the lyric generation, in having so few children, had acted indeed in such a way as to conserve their position in society and to protect themselves from those who might one day pose a threat to that position. Not to procreate, or to procreate so little that its offspring would always be inferior in number and therefore in strength, certainly constitutes for a generation the best way of not finding itself overwhelmed, challenged, and eventually obliged to cede its place. Contrary to popular wisdom, it is the *lack* of children and young people around adults that prevents the latter from aging, not their presence. For youth then continues to be their possession, and no one can wrest it from them.

That said, the denial of procreation is not the only way

the refusal to be a parent can express itself. Nor is it the most effective way, for there will always be births, despite everything. Three representative cases may be cited in this regard. (1) The new adult has had one or two children at the very beginning of the marriage, unthinkingly or through carelessness, before "discovering himself" and taking his life in hand; this frequently happened towards the end of the sixties. (2) The day arrives, just before turning forty, when the need to "realize oneself fully as a woman or a man" leads one to live the experience of maternity or paternity before it is too late: that is what the Americans call the "baby-boom echo." (3) Finally — and this is the new trend, which applies perforce only to men — a man marries a woman twenty years his junior and makes her the generous offer of his name and semen, so as not to frustrate her in her youth and because she adores babies. And so most adults of this generation will have ended up reproducing, despite themselves.

But to reproduce is not necessarily to be a parent. Just as their childhood and youth were reinvented, unfolding in such a way that they took on meanings totally foreign to the childhood and youth of earlier generations, so these adults would reinvent and utterly transform the secular condition of being a parent. Or rather, they would invent the art of being a parent, without being a parent at all, which is a pure marvel.

This art, thoroughly typical of the young life, consists in having children, feeding them, raising them, spoiling them even, but without in any way being burdened by them or deprived of the freedom to desire, change, fulfil oneself — in short, to be young. In former times, being a parent consisted primarily in a search for order and stability. Parents worked hard to erect a rampart of continuity, permanence, and solidity around their fragile and mercurial children and adolescents. Their role, they thought, was to protect the temporarily unstable lives of their sons and daughters, who were still vulnerable and uncertain, while living their own lives in as peaceful and stable a fashion as they could manage.

Naturally, such abnegation represented, for the new breed of parents, just the opposite of what they expected from life and what life was supposed to expect from them. It also represented the opposite of what they expected of their children, and what they assumed their children expected or ought to have expected from life: the perpetual euphoria that alone could inspire the rejection of all alienating structures, of any restraint on the full self-realization of each of the "partners."

After all, why must a parent be a slave to that role? Before being a father or mother, was I not first of all an individual? Did I not have the right to satisfy my desires? Was it not my duty to develop my faculties to their utmost, to realize fully my potential for happiness? Why should I close myself off? Why, in pursuing my life in this union, should I consent to be frustrated, not to fulfil myself, to sacrifice what I am? Why, in short, should the new parents continue to do what their own parents did simply because they had no choice: to resign themselves to being parents and to grow old?

Besides, it is not good for children to have a mother or father who is not at peace with her- or himself. And then, to have two parents, or always the same mother, or always the same father, is not always advisable. The children might be overprotected, apathetic, less well prepared to deal with the challenges their lives and careers will inevitably place in their way. Their feeling of autonomy — the most precious attribute a small child today can possibly offer his or her parents, just as those of yore made their parents happy by being docile or well-behaved — might even be compromised.

And so the new art of parenthood favoured a profusion of unprecedented models, ranging from the "divided" family to the "shared" or "reconstituted" family, and including varieties no less new of "childhood experiences" and parent-child "contracts," each more interesting and promising than the next. Not all the bugs, of course, have been worked out of the system. Like any revolution, this one must first pass through a transitional stage during which a certain amount of damage is done. There is no liberation without suffering. For the moment, it is the men who are experiencing the most success in this new art. They are even succeeding with remarkable ease, so much so that the burden of this transition, known as single parenthood and double duty, has fallen almost entirely on women. While, and doubtless because, their companions have been able to blithely reconcile fatherhood with bachelorhood and fatherhood with eternal youth, women continue to be hampered, if not imprisoned, by the bonds of their maternity, which are even more onerous and painful because they bear them alone and are alone required to abandon, limit, or defer their own liberation.

Women, however, are not the only victims, nor even, perhaps, the most deeply affected. More difficult still, would seem to be the fate of many children and adolescents conscripted despite themselves into this revolution in family values. Because in reality, and this is less paradoxical than it might seem at first sight, a young society is a society where there is no longer any place for childhood, just as there is no longer any place for maturity and old age. These two exclusions are closely linked, in fact, in that they both derive from the lightening of the world and its disappearance as a horizon and perimeter for existence. For if the old embodied a willingness to accept the weight and presence of the world, children represented the need, urge, and opportunity for renewal. In the one case the world's continuation was expressed through its past, in the other, in anticipation and uncertainty; in the first, mortality had been momentarily overcome, in the second it revived and demanded to be dealt with anew.

But when there is no more world to be borne, when nothing that preceded my life must endure, why should anything survive me? The child, by his very presence, through the stability and seniority that he expects of me, thrusts me inexorably into old age. He removes me from myself, prevents me from doing with my life what I please, fossilizes me, denies me, condemns me to being in his eyes just one more actor in the world, just an instrument of the past. When it comes to living the young life, when it comes to the young life's privileges and obligations, a child is always surplus baggage.

This is clearly seen in the ideologies and practices that today dominate the field of education. Celebrated far and wide by a whole legion of school administrators, family therapists, psychologists, and other child experts specializing in the pedagogical sciences, the new models for education have only one end in view: the happiness and self-fulfilment of the little ones. But since it is always up to adults to define these things, the meaning will be determined by the adults of the lyric generation, and it will be a meaning that coincides perfectly with their own idea of happiness and fulfilment: a softening of demands and constraints, a distrust of any imposed structure that might devalue or inhibit the child, the encouragement of spontaneous competences and natural creativity, and so on. The idea is to ask as little as possible of the child, to be attentive to him, to let him develop at his own pace, without forcing anything, without intimidating, and, above all, without requiring him to act older than his age or understand what he does not yet have to understand. Let him play, watch television, express himself, enjoy his childhood, and nature will take care of the rest. In short, let him remain a child.

Let him remain a child and leave us in peace. For the first to profit from this liberation of education is not, of course, the child, who has no need of liberation — liberation from what? — but rather the adult, the parent, or the teacher, who is once more absolved of any obligation to grow old, in other words, to embody and assume responsibility for the world in the eyes of those young people who are asking to be allowed in. Responsibility for the world as a presence that is already there, as a territory that has been structured beforehand, and therefore, indeed, as *authority*. But the world also as a *shared dwelling place,* as a promise and an exaction. The traditional role of education has been not only to have children and adolescents submit to the customs and traditions of adults. It has also been, first and foremost, to embrace them and place the world in their hands, that they might live in it and transform it.

Now a so-called liberated education, based on a supposed respect for the child, confines the child or adolescent to a world apart, a cross between a playpen and a concentration camp, with no access to the world outside. To demand nothing of him, to avoid *teaching* him anything, and to ask him to *discover* everything by himself on the pretext of preparing him for a new world, is to restrict him to his own life and his own experiences, and so to conformity and boredom. It is to refuse him the means to innovate, to stand up to adults, to contest their authority, and therefore, ulti-mately, to change the world. Under cover of liberating him, we isolate him and deprive him of the opportunity to gain access one day to a shared world, to measure himself by it, and to transform it.

It is through an awareness of the world's great age, in other words, and by ensuring that the world as *past* be handed on, that education can offer to children and adolescents the world as *future*. But to assume responsibility for the past and to hand it down would require me to be accountable, myself, for what has gone before and to entrust the future to others. It would require me to vacate my place, to step aside, to leave to the young that eternal youth that was accorded me.

To say goodbye forever to the enchanted island of Daphnis. To lose myself in the world.

EPILOGUE

We were born never to grow
old, never to die.

Raoul Vaneigem
*A Treatise on How to Live
for the Use of Young Generations*

Although it is euphoric, the young life is nevertheless not without anxiety. For there comes, inevitably, a moment when youth cannot be taken for granted and requires, on the contrary, effort and concentration to overcome the increasing threat of the body's disintegration, sickness, and eventual death. Narcissus, stubbornly crouched above his pool, has not seen time pass; one morning he is astonished to discover himself mortal, and he is disconcerted.

The signs of this anxiety begin to appear as we embark upon the final decades of our lives. They take the form now of regret, disorientation, and fear, now of a kind of frenzy laced with forgetfulness, now again of an eternal youth that has somehow become burdensome. It is sometimes pathetic, sometimes laughable. But whichever it is, we can be sure that these signs will become more and more evident as the anxiety deepens.

And it can only deepen. For however certain our disappearance, it is something we have become unable to imagine. Only the adult, only the aged, only he who has submitted to the world can conceive of what it must be to decline and die. But how can the "new" adult of the lyric generation assume his own mortality? When faced with this last obstacle that he has denied right to the end, that he has fended off for as long as possible, but that will be, now, inescapable, how will he ever *recognize* himself? How will he transgress death?

All we know for the moment, and we know it absolutely, is that the decline and fall of this generation will again occur in great numbers. It will once more be a phenomenon of great magnitude, rapid and concentrated in time. There will be a wave of terminal illnesses and deaths, during which power will be in the hands of the sick and dying.

We can foresee, as well, as we might suspect from recent developments in euthanasia and the right to die with dignity, that the procedures for dying will be eased. And so perhaps will be vanquished the last possible thralldom to the world, the obligation to experience the burdens of physical suffering and the pangs of death.

But death itself, the reality of stillness and eclipse, how will we reinvent it? What will it resemble, a "lyric death"?

INDEX

consent, 213–214
conservation, 171, 236–238
conservatism, 44–46, 193
constraints
    lack of on lyric generation
        in childhood, 61–68
        during youth, 73, 76–80, 93–94,
            97–110
    and lyric generation mentality, 155, 173,
        179, 233, 241
    and non-lyric generations, 98, 145,
        250–251
constraints. *See also* desire(s); freedom; limits;
    resistance
consumption/consumerism, 93–94,
    204–205, 227–237, 241
content, absence of, 218, 220, 223, 224, 233
contestation, 124
continuity, 135, 146, 158–159, 170, 193,
    244, 247, 249
contraception. *See* birth control
control
    and lyric generation adults, 153–164, 166,
        171, 181
    and lyric generation youth, 153–154
control. *See also* authority; constraints;
    freedom; influence; power
conviction, morality of, 157
counterculture, 187
creativity, 103, 187, 250–251
criticism, 124, 167, 181, 188, 189
crowds, 130–131, 134, 135, 136, 210
culture
    and identity, 132
    ideologies of, 181–182, 183, 186, 187–190
    and lyric generation adults, 159, 165,
        182–183, 186, 216, 221–222, 231,
        245
    and lyric generation youth, 73
    and pre-lyric generations, 13, 81
Czechoslovakia, 94, 126

day care, 159, 160
death/dying, 121, 186, 253, 254
de Beauvoir, Simone, 184
Debray, Régis, 200, 203
decadence, 100, 101
deconstruction, 186
de Gaulle, Charles, 126
demands
    and lyric generation adults, 155, 192, 202,
        204, 207, 210–211, 220, 228, 229
    and post-lyric generations, 250–251
demands. *See also* student movement
democracy/democratization, 132, 203,
    205–206, 210, 221

demographers, 28, 30–31, 46
demographic equilibrium, 6–7, 24–25, 33,
    42, 75, 171–173, 244. *See also* age
    pyramid; population composition
demoralization, 106, 143
demystification, 187, 188–189
denial, 167, 171, 233. *See also* limits
dependence, 74–75, 118, 156
depersonalization, 137
Depression
    effects of, 12, 13, 14, 17, 22, 37–38, 81,
        100
    relationship of to baby boom, 29, 30,
        37–38, 74
Depression generation, 81, 84–87, 91
desanctification of politics/the state,
    196–197, 202–203, 211, 213
Desbiens, Jean-Paul, 87
desire(s)
    and baby boom/lyric generation, 19, 45,
        66, 218
    and lyric generation adults, 155, 157, 173,
        177, 178, 193, 200, 208, 228, 229,
        232, 233, 235, 237, 241, 242, 248
    and lyric generation youth, 94, 100, 107,
        108, 146, 147
    and non-lyric generations, 15, 79, 144,
        145, 147
desire(s). *See also* constraints; freedom
despair, 16–17, 106, 110
despotic state, 206–207
destiny, 72, 76
destruction, 19, 167, 177, 185–187
discourse, 178, 223–225. *See also* ideologies
discovery, 154, 251
"discretionary social behaviour," 176–177,
    182
discrimination, 125
disenchantment, 187, 194
disgust, 102
disintellectualizing, 187
disorientation, 106, 253
disposable income, 229–230
dispossession, 221–222
dissatisfaction, 101, 143
dissent, 157
distinctiveness, 23, 45
distinct society, 211
disturbance, TV avoids creating any, 220,
    222
disturbance/disruption, 42, 50, 68, 71, 220,
    222. *See also* rupture
diversion, ideology as, 176–177
diversity, 183
divinity, 142, 167
divorce, 38, 159

domestication of politics, 195–211, 214
dreams, 143, 155, 186
drugs, 135, 136, 137, 180, 193
Ducharme, Réjean, 87
Duplessis, Maurice, 82, 84

Eastern mysticism, 179
ecology/ecological thought, 235–236, 237–238
economic activity. *See* consumption
economic growth. *See* prosperity
economicism, 193
economic status, 52, 93–94, 163
economy
of consumption, 227–237
and later baby boom, 49, 51
and lyric generation, 51, 55, 56, 169, 245
and lyric generation adults, 156, 230–231
and lyric generation youth, 113
education, 230
and lyric generation adults, 156, 158, 176, 242, 245
and lyric generation as children/youth, 55, 62–68, 74–75, 92–93, 112–113, 115–117, 126, 146, 155, 159, 175–176, 245
and post-lyric generations, 250–251
and pre-lyric generations, 205
and television/mass media, 215, 216, 220, 221–222, 224
education. *See also* student movement
ego, 129
eighties, and lyric generation adults, 154, 175, 177–178, 180, 194
elders. *See* age/aging; Depression generation; old; parents
elites/elitism, 66–67, 83, 109, 114, 215
emancipatory movements, 122–123
emotional climate, 101–110
employment, 51–52, 74–75, 92–93, 159, 161, 162–163. *See also* work
end, the, obsession with, 185–187
energy, 102, 157, 159
English Canada, 37, 43
ennui, 101–102, 177, 235
enragés, 123
entertainment, 159, 216, 220
enthusiasm, 103, 184, 187, 195, 209, 227, 228
entitlement, 94, 229
entrepreneurship, 156, 163
environment, 236
Enzenberger, Hans-Magnus, 218
Enzenberger hypothesis, 213–225, 233
ephemeral, the, 168, 171
epigones, 183–184
escape, 216, 222, 233, 240

establishment, 125–126, 191
eternity/the eternal, 168, 171, 233
ethos, 166, 171, 173, 243
euphoria
and lyric generation adults, 167, 210, 218, 232, 239, 248, 253
and lyric generation youth, 119, 125, 134
euphoria. *See also* joy
euthanasia, 254
exaltation, 99, 102, 105, 106
excitement, 105
exile, 86, 101
existence, 239, 241
existential climate, and lyric generation's birth, 11–19, 23, 48–49
existential crises, and non-lyric generations, 142–143
expectations
and lyric generation adults, 155, 157, 158, 171, 173, 195, 207, 220, 228, 242, 245, 248
and lyric generation youth, 71, 74, 92
and post-lyric generations, 52
and pre-lyric generations, 14, 15, 155
expectations. *See also* hope
experience, 144, 148
exploitation, and post-lyric generations, 52
Expo 67, 134, 136
extremism, 120

failure, 145, 147
faith
and lyric generation adults, 167, 177, 178, 241
and lyric generation youth, 120, 135, 141
and pre-lyric generations, 13, 16, 146, 199
family
and lyric generation adults, 245, 248–249
and lyric generation childhood, 23–24, 63–64
fascism, 199
fashion, 94, 103, 228, 230
fatherhood, 247, 249–250
fear, 236–237, 253
fellowship. *See* belonging; community
feminine mystique, 36
feminism, 36, 37, 182–183, 185, 194
fertility, 32, 35
festivals, 133–137, 209–210
fidelity, 241
Fifth Republic, 94
fifties, 170, 215–216
film, 43, 181, 221, 224
firstborns
of baby boom, 47, 49, 53
in lyric generation, 49